M000028210

# The Myth of International Protection

CALIFORNIA SERIES IN PUBLIC
ANTHROPOLOGY

The California Series in Public Anthropology
emphasizes the anthropologist's role as an
engaged intellectual. It continues anthropology's
commitment to being an ethnographic witness,
to describing, in human terms, how life is lived
beyond the borders of many readers' experiences. But it also adds a commitment, through
ethnography, to reframing the terms of public
debate—transforming received, accepted understandings of social issues with new insights, new
framings.

*Series Editor: Robert Borofsky (Hawaii Pacific
University)*

*Contributing Editors: Philippe Bourgois (University of
Pennsylvania), Paul Farmer (Partners In Health),
Alex Hinton (Rutgers University), Carolyn Nordstrom
(University of Notre Dame), and Nancy Scheper-
Hughes (UC Berkeley)*

*University of California Press Editor: Naomi
Schneider*

# The Myth of International Protection

## Protection

*War and Survival in Congo*

Claudia Seymour

UNIVERSITY OF CALIFORNIA PRESS

University of California Press, one of the most distinguished university presses in the United States, enriches lives around the world by advancing scholarship in the humanities, social sciences, and natural sciences. Its activities are supported by the UC Press Foundation and by philanthropic contributions from individuals and institutions. For more information, visit www.ucpress.edu.

University of California Press
Oakland, California

© 2019 by Claudia Seymour

Library of Congress Cataloging-in-Publication Data

Names: Seymour, Claudia, 1976- author.
Title: The myth of international protection : war and
    survival in Congo / Claudia Seymour.
Description: Oakland, California : University of
    California Press, [2019] | Series: California series in
    public anthropology | Includes bibliographical
    references and index. |
Identifiers: LCCN 2018037835 (print) | LCCN 2018042618
    (ebook) | ISBN 9780520971417 (ebook) |
    ISBN 9780520299832 (cloth : alk. paper) |
    ISBN 9780520299849 (paperback)
Subjects: LCSH: International relief—Congo (Democratic
    Republic) | Child welfare—International cooperation.
    | Children and violence—Congo (Democratic
    Republic)
Classification: LCC HV455.5 (EBOOK) | LCC HV455.5 .S49 2019
    (PRINT) | DDC 362.7—dc23
LC record available at http://lccn.loc.gov/2018037835

Manufactured in the United States of America

28  27  26  25  24  23  22  21  20  19
10  9  8  7  6  5  4  3  2  1

*For Byamungu, Emile, Hadjiana, François,*
*Machozi, and Vainqueur*
*For their children*
*For Leo*

Every injury whatever,
The whole variety of evil deeds
Is brought about by circumstances.
None is independent, none autonomous.

Shantideva, *The Way of
the Bodhisattva* (c. 700 CE)

# CONTENTS

*Acknowledgments*  ix

*List of Abbreviations*  xii

*Map*  xiv

1. A Beginning

1

2. Outrages in Congo

18

3. Surviving Violence

42

4. Embodying Violence

58

5. Navigating Violence

83

6. Meanings of Violence
108

7. The Myth of International Protection
130

*Notes   145*

*References   157*

*Index   169*

# ACKNOWLEDGMENTS

To all the Congolese people who opened their lives to me and who shared their stories, I am profoundly indebted. I am especially grateful to Lebon Mulimbi of Action pour la Protection des Droits Humains et de Développement Communautaire and the team in Bunyakiri, including Idriss Bengibabuya, Byamungu Mutongo, Vainqueur Chikuru Mapenzi, Pascasie Nakamosi Chipere, Mapendo Lambaira, Rehema, Machozi, Pacifique Zakariya Bikulongabo, and Jolie Bengibabuya Milabyo. I thank the directors and staff of Laissez l'Afrique Vivre, l'Action pour la Paix et la Concorde, and Cris d'Afrique in South Kivu and the staff of War Child UK, War Child Holland, and Save the Children UK for facilitating parts of this research. Telesphore Kanyamulera, Gaspard Kisoki Sumaili, Pascal Mugula, and Blaise Rugemintore were sources of knowledge and wisdom. To John Saidi, who died in 2008: may his dreams of a better future for his children one day soon come true.

My greatest fortune was to have Zoë Marriage as my PhD supervisor. With intellectual rigor, saintly patience, and endless generosity, she has guided and supported me on so many life dimensions. The School of Oriental and African Studies is an exceptional institution; in the Department of Development Studies, Tania Kaiser, Christopher Cramer, Laura Hammond, and Alfredo Saad-Filho deserve special thanks. I am grateful to Jason Hart, Philip Clark, and Johan Pottier, who devoted their time and wisdom to making me a better researcher. At the Graduate Institute of International and Development Studies in Geneva, I thank Oliver Jütersonke, Sandra Patricia Reimann, Keith Krause, and Achim Wennmann for their support.

This book would have probably never been written without the constant support and encouragement of Robert Borofsky of the Center for a Public Anthropology—his belief in this project for more than a decade kept me going when I otherwise might have given up. I am grateful to Naomi Schneider and Benjy Malings at the University of California Press for their support and guidance, to Susan Ecklund for her precise and patient copyediting, and to the California Series in Public Anthropology for its commitment to addressing the challenges facing us all. My gratitude goes to Michael Wessells, Christopher Cramer, and the two anonymous reviewers whose insights have made this book so much better than it otherwise would have been. I thank the extremely talented Miriam Nabarro for her art on the cover of this book, Sean Bennett for his map, and Vainqueur Mapenzi for sharing his artwork.

Over the many years it took to write this book, I was nourished, refuged, and supported by cherished friends, including Sara Mancell, Caroline Appel, Lindsay Bush, Alessandra Campanaro, Josefin Holmberg, Sophia Swithern, Emilie Medeiros, Zabhia Youssef, Alexandra MacDowall, Isabella Phoenix, Imogen Prickett, Vanessa Kent, Juana de Catheu, Darcy Roehling, and Wendy

MacClinchy. Mayling Birney, who gave so many of us so much, lives on in spirit. I have been fortunate to have Fatuma Ibrahim, Wayne Bleier, Saudamini Seigrist, Angela Kearney, Gilbert Khadiagala, and Colin Scott as guides. I also thank the healers who kept me going: Mary Foley, Eve Khambhatta, Starling Gifford, Sarah Gamble, and Mukti Elisabeth Talumière. I am grateful to my yoga community in Annecy, as well as to LakeAid, the French Red Cross, and the MJC Romains for allowing me to continue my work very close to home.

My parents, Luz Adiela Seymour Salazar and Arthur Seymour, and my sister, Rosemary Urness, will always have my deepest gratitude. Diego and Gladys Salazar, Nadia Ferrari, and Gabriele Giusta have been core sources of support and encouragement. Marco Cordero accompanied this long journey with honesty and integrity and gave me the greatest of all gifts: Leo, to whom I dedicate it all.

# ABBREVIATIONS

| | |
|---|---|
| AFDL | Alliance des Forces Démocratiques pour la Libération du Congo |
| ALiR | Armée de Liberation du Rwanda |
| ANC | Armée Nationale Congolaise |
| CNDP | Congrès National pour la Défense du Peuple |
| DDR | disarmament, demobilization, and reintegration |
| DRC | Democratic Republic of the Congo |
| EITI | Extractive Industries Transparency Initiative |
| FAR | Forces Armées Rwandaises |
| FARDC | Forces Armées de la République Démocratique du Congo |
| FAZ | Forces Armées Zairoises |
| FDLR | Forces démocratiques de libération du Rwanda |
| ICRC | International Committee of the Red Cross |
| LUCHA | Lutte pour le Changement |

| | |
|---|---|
| MONUC | Mission de l'Organisation des Nations Unies en République démocratique du Congo |
| MONUSCO | Mission de l'Organisation des Nations Unies pour la stabilisation en République démocratique du Congo |
| MRM | Monitoring and Reporting Mechanism |
| M23 | Mouvement du 23 mars |
| M40 | Mudundu 40 |
| NGO | nongovernmental organization |
| PTSD | post-traumatic stress disorder |
| RCD | Rassemblement Congolais pour la Démocratie |
| RPA | Rwandan Patriotic Army |
| UN | United Nations |
| UNICEF | United Nations Children's Fund |

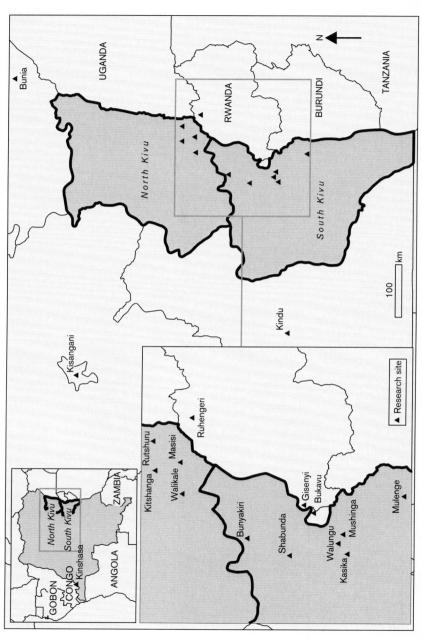

Map of research sites. Credit: Sean Bennett.

# CHAPTER ONE

# A Beginning

## ARRIVALS

I first arrived in the Democratic Republic of the Congo (DRC) in early 2006, deployed as a child protection adviser to the United Nations (UN) peacekeeping mission. Having just completed a posting in war-ravaged Liberia, I had already witnessed the impacts of terrible violence and destruction. While I had experienced the positive potential of international aid interventions in conflict zones, I had also been confronted by their failures. My faith in the capacity of an individual to "do good" in the world was slightly shaken, but I was not yet ready to surrender it. Still hopeful, I was intent on continuing my quest into the darkness of humanity, trusting that, in the end, light would be found, and good could be done.

If any country needed good, it was the DRC. It had just emerged from a devastating war fought on a continental scale. Millions of Congolese people had died directly and indirectly from the violence.[1] Following more than a century of misrule

*country ravaged by war*

and violent exploitation, the DRC was one of the poorest countries in the world. When I arrived there, life expectancy at birth was barely fifty years, while health care and other basic services were almost entirely absent throughout large parts of the country. Atrocious human development indicators belied the DRC's extreme natural resource wealth.

In the first decade of the twenty-first century, the DRC hosted the world's largest international peacekeeping mission.[2] My rapid indoctrination to UN peacekeeping started in Kinshasa, the vibrant but decrepit Congolese capital. My early days in the DRC were a blur of meetings, briefings, and security orientations, as I navigated the bewildering administration that churned behind high white-and-blue, barbed-wire-topped walls. On my third day in the country, I was informed that I would be dispatched to Kisangani to manage the UN mission's child protection mandate in the two eastern provinces of Orientale and Maniema. I took to peering at my freshly printed maps and to burying myself as deeply and quickly as I could into the available history of eastern DRC.

Through this early orientation, I learned that the city of Kisangani, nestled in the vastness of the Congo Basin forest, had been administratively established in 1883 as a trading hub under Belgium's King Leopold II. Before independence from Belgium in 1960, Kisangani had served as a center of Patrice Lumumba's anticolonial resistance movement. In 1964, the Simba rebellion against the Western-supported government in Kinshasa—one of the many Cold War transpositions on the African continent—based its military operations out of Kisangani, drawing on reserves of soldiers and mercenaries of all nations and presaging the entrenched internationalism of Congolese wars. In the post–Cold War era, Kisangani would again witness catastrophic

"Africa's World War"[3]

violence. During the 1996–2003 wars—what Gérard Prunier would term "Africa's World War"—thousands of civilians perished as Uganda and Rwanda fought for control of the lucrative eastern region.[3] The UN peacekeeping mission that I had just joined was still endeavoring to piece the country back together after those wars.

It did not take me long to appreciate how such a violent history becomes manifest in the present. In places so destroyed by war, so cut off from any prospect of economic development, people were left to fend for themselves as services and support systems decayed all around them. With their poverty constantly closing in, people had little recourse but to express fury. Quick eruptions of mob violence occurred regularly in Kisangani. More than once, John—my long-suffering, devoted, and now departed Congolese colleague—would save me from a rock-throwing crowd poised to hijack any passing white UN Land Cruiser, shouting at me to close my window, lock my door, and drive through the crowd or make a quick U-turn to escape.

By 2006, the front lines of conflict had at last receded from Kisangani's sprawling streets. In their place, urban misery had encroached, appropriating any hope for peace and bringing chronic desolation. Destroyed by the war and asphyxiated by the absence of infrastructure that could sustain legitimate trade, the local economy of Kisangani was devastated. Consequently, the social supports that had held life together so precariously during the many decades of extreme hardship were now barely holding on.

local economy + social supports of Kisangani devastated

One obvious indicator of this failing social system was the rapidly rising population of street children. By 2006, their numbers in Kisangani had swelled, as children living in households on the furthest edges of precarity were pushed out of their homes, blamed by adults for all possible household hardships, from AIDS to the breakdown of families, to the suffocating impossibility of meeting daily survival needs. With no recourse but to their own capacities to navigate the streets of Kisangani, these children would become an important focus of my child protection efforts there. I followed them into the depths of postwar misery, where accusations of modern witchcraft flourished. I convened meetings with parents, pastors, and community leaders; organized radio awareness campaigns; mobilized lawyers; and conducted count-less visits to church compounds where extreme torture was being sold as exorcism by profiteering pastors.

I exhausted all available possibilities to convince those I met that children must not be sacrificed in reaction to all that had come before them. But the tides had long since risen, and I could not help these children. In my personal journal, I documented one of uncounted moments of hopelessness I confronted in the streets of Kisangani:

> 19 November 2006: Sunday night. I light a candle in honour of La Vie, the corpse of the boy we uncovered this morning. His body, mutilated by the black-gray scars of a hot iron, was already starting to swell in the heat of the midmorning sun. How old had he been? Maybe seventeen? No one knew. A child of the street, mourned in trembling wails by his street sisters, by the angry tears and clenched fists of his street brothers—to everyone else, his was a life worth nothing. Shuttling between the morgue, the mayor, the funeral pro-cession, through the Kisangani streets down to the river, we laid his body in a pirogue to cross the river Congo—to the home of a father who had so long ago abandoned his son—to its final resting place.

Within me, such poverty and helplessness transformed into anger and an overwhelming sense of defeat. My time in Kisangani was hot and hard and left me without any feeling of satisfaction in a job well done. But before these grim expressions of humanity's hardship could extinguish what was left of my faith, UN human resources took over. I was to be urgently redeployed to Goma, where emergency child protection support was needed in response to the resurging conflict there.

## DOCUMENTING VIOLENCE: AN INTRODUCTION

My first glimpse of North Kivu came through the small, round window of an Antonov aircraft. We landed with a jarring bump, not far from the active Nyiragongo volcano. A rainstorm had just passed, and the mist rose from the warm earth in a prism of late afternoon sunlight. The erupting landscape of Goma was unlike any place I had ever been. Its penetrating natural beauty had—I would learn—humbling power over life and death. A land of extremes, the Kivus would reveal to me the very worst and the very best of the human experience. There, I would learn the limits of my own capacity.

Minutes later, I arrived at the UN base, just across the street from the airport. The tension and uncertainty were palpable; it was 22 November 2006, and Goma was very close to being seized by the current main rebel force. Although various peace deals had been negotiated to end the war at a national level by 2003, the incredible natural resource wealth of the Kivus meant that there remained too much to gain from conflict and too much to lose from peace. The logics of violence thus continued to govern, as armed groups served local, national, regional, and, above all, commercial interests, while the languishing population fled, submitted, and sank deeper into its misery.

Walking across the volcanic gravel toward my assigned container-cum-office, I was met by Luis, the head of the UN human rights section, as he emerged from his dust-covered Land Cruiser.[4] He and his team of human rights officers were just arriving from the small town of Rutshuru, where they had traveled to document a recent massacre. Exhaustion grayed their faces, but they incarnated a bound-up energy and a clear-sighted sense of purpose. "Ah, Claudia! Welcome to Goma. We're glad you're here." Luis took my hand in his with warmth, then continued in his next breath: "We're just back. It was horrific. Women, head first in latrines, stomachs lacerated. We need to go write this up. Let's talk later?"

I had arrived in Goma. Like the colleagues I had just met, I would very soon become mired in the dark extremes of human possibilities. My own work would focus on grave human rights abuses against children. The gruesome potential of what people can do to each other would become the substance of my days. The suffering and pain I would witness were beyond anything I had ever fathomed. I would document these atrocities until late at night, then send my reports on to Kinshasa. Sometimes, some of the details I had written would be included in the daily dispatches to New York, to be read as part of a morning briefing over coffee.

I quickly immersed myself in the pulsing beat of the Kivus, and it was only a matter of days before I was consumed by the same agitation, rage, and focus that I had sensed in my first meeting with Luis. I became absorbed in the terribleness of it all. There was no time to think, only to react, to decry, to move faster, to try to stanch the endless flow of abuses. Another journal entry, written two months after my arrival in Goma:

> 19 January 2007: How to wash away the pain? Her tears? The memory of her smell, a rank mix of blood, urine, semen. The odor of her fear that still hangs everywhere around me—I can taste it. Helpless

but trying to help, I bring her to the hospital, and finally leave her there. Later, I recount this day to [my supervisor] in Kinshasa over the phone. She hears and advises, and then suggests that I take a shower once home, "not a bath. You cannot sit in this," she says. "You must wash this day off so that you can keep going."

Of course, my supervisor knew that such feelings never wash off, not really, that the only way to continue to do this kind of work is to be fully steeped in it, to embody it, to work harder and more extremely, to push all possible limits.

My days in Goma were incredibly intense, but also uniquely fulfilling. Working in a zone of active conflict made every action—and nonaction—seem consequential. Each day was so full of new emergencies: forced child recruitment to armed groups, sexual violence, abductions. Each violation was to be investigated, referred, then documented. The frenetic energy made it feel like I was doing something, that my actions were making a difference.

But even as I pushed through each day, each report, something began to nag at my conscience. My professional title was child protection adviser, yet I was increasingly unable to deny just how little "protection" I was providing. I could not stop the terrible acts of violence, only document them. I could advocate and follow up, but I could not prevent the abuses from happening in the first place. While I understood on a conceptual level that there was a role to be played in making such terrible abuses known to the wider world in the hopes that this knowledge might one day generate enough political will to end them, I was mostly overwhelmed by a sense of defeat. I often felt like an accountant, enumerating violences, counting horrors that I could do nothing to stop. I held on to a belief that writing down this human suffering would somehow contribute to its end.

Later, I would read the work of political economist David Keen, who described the futile and dehumanizing act of amassing "catalogues of human rights abuses" and who noted the inconsequential change that usually results.[5] My discomfort grew, and once I allowed myself to examine my unease more deeply, I began to understand that there was something wrong about the fight in which I was engaged. The stark contradiction between the absolutist discourse of "inalienable rights" and the daily reality of abuse experienced by most people became too much for me to ignore. The more carefully I listened, the more I could hear the historical depth, political complexity, and global interdependence of the violence against which I was so desperately trying to protect children.

Yet in a context of "humanitarian emergency" and "rapid response," there was no time for reflection, for questioning, or for understanding. There was no space for complexity. Another journal entry, a month later:

> 20 February 2007: Last night, shots fired off again, this time in quick succession, somewhere very nearby. Silence. I turned off my light, then laid, taut in attention, ready to flee, white currents pulsing in the arches of my feet. I searched the shadows then realized that it's the shadows I don't know enough, that I must learn to know if I am to survive here. Sound, sight, then smell.... I could smell another body, but then nothing, then realized it was the smell of my fear, clad in fetid army green, unwashed and overused and dangerously powerless. Finally, eventually, I fell asleep, and now I wake to this new day, not with courage, but exhaustion. I'm not on solid ground anymore. Nothing is as it first seems.

Even as the battles continued to wage never very far away, I was reasonably safe. Just like the thousands of privileged others endeavoring to "do good" in the DRC, I lived behind high walls, was escorted and secured. Unlike the millions of Congolese who welcomed us, we could escape when the situation became too difficult or too compromised.

## LEAVING, RETURNING

Eventually it was time for me to leave, but even as I boarded my outbound flight from Kinshasa, I was already planning my return. I was heading to London, where I would begin doctoral research under the supervision of Dr. Zoë Marriage at the School of Oriental and African Studies. Zoë quickly became my guiding light, and with her I began sorting through my experiences in the DRC, trying to make some theoretical sense out of what I had seen and lived. Many of my early hours with Zoë involved her listening deeply and questioning patiently. From my mind-set of impassioned reactivity—This is terrible! We must do something!—she steered me toward a more reflective mode that would instead wonder: Interesting, why does this keep happening?

I considered the questions I wanted to answer and then elaborated the research methods that would guide my fieldwork. I immersed myself in the literatures of anthropology, political economy, psychology, and sociology as they related to violence across time and geographic space. I was influenced especially by the ethnographic work of Philippe Bourgois, who showed through his research—decades earlier and continents away—that violence does not simply disappear, is not merely survived, but is transformed and incorporated into our ways of perceiving, being in, and re-creating the world.[6] Eventually I decided that the goal of my research would be to understand young people's experiences not just of the terrible violences of war but also of their everydays, of their processes of coping and ways of simply getting on with life, despite the violence everywhere around them.

Over the course of the following decade, I would return to the DRC in varying professional and research capacities. In 2009, I served with the UN Security Council–mandated Group of Experts on the DRC to support investigations into grave human rights violations.[7] Beginning in late 2009, my focus turned to ethnographic research with young people. I alternated between periods of fieldwork as a student and—to pay for my studies—as a researcher commissioned by various international nongovernmental organizations (NGOs), including Save the Children UK, War Child Holland and War Child UK, and Oxfam GB. Later, I would travel to the DRC as a researcher with the Small Arms Survey, and then for the USAID–Education in Crisis and Conflict Network.

Throughout, I relied primarily on qualitative research methods, including interviews, group discussions, and participant observation. My priority was to ensure that the research could be safely conducted while creating as few risks as possible to my research participants and collaborators. In those years foreign researchers were rarely targeted or attacked in the DRC (regrettably, this is no longer the case), yet the participants or the individuals supporting me could have been threatened. I carefully weighed the risks and anticipated harms involved with the research and anchored my methods not only in the Ethical Guidelines for Good Research Practice of the Association of Social Anthropologists of the UK and the Commonwealth but also in international child protection standards and guidelines specific to conducting research with children in contexts of violent conflict.[8]

Between 2006 and 2016, approximately two thousand people directly informed this research.[9] They came from villages and cities throughout the Kivus, Orientale, or Maniema or else lived in Kinshasa and neighboring Rwanda. They included young people, their parents, local leaders, religious actors, military commanders, demobilized soldiers, government authorities, and my professional colleagues. These individuals were the vital force that drove my research; their narratives form the cornerstone of this book.

My extended period of fieldwork and repeat visits to the DRC provided me the opportunity to conduct truly grounded research. Multiple phases of fieldwork spread over several years allowed me to fully engage with the relevant theoretical literatures across disciplines and to then weave this theory back into the experiences of life in the DRC. Some of my young Congolese research participants were eager to engage with and challenge the concepts and theoretical constructs that I would bring back to them. As such, this book documents an iterative and organic process of theory influencing my understanding of violence influencing my engagement with theory, and on it continues.[10]

The insights and knowledge provided by my Congolese research participants continue to infuse my ongoing work with young people far beyond the DRC. My theoretical engagement with Pierre Bourdieu's law of conservation of violence—which examines how violence is reproduced through social, political, economic, cultural, and historic structures—influences my current research with young people not only in other conflict settings but also on the margins of European society today.[11] By tracing trajectories of violence, and by considering the pathways through which violence is conserved by society and by individuals, it becomes possible to see how, for example, ongoing conflict and adversity lead to migration outflows, which lead to populist fear-based political rhetoric in destination countries, which leads to exclusion, which leads to deeper inequalities, which lead to continuing violence. And on it can go without end.

### TRANSFORMING VIOLENCE?

Like electricity, violence follows the path of least resistance, transmitted not only in the relationships between people and their immediate social structures, from one person to the next, from one generation to the next, but also through the global economic systems in which we are all embedded. According to Bourdieu, as long as the social, political, and economic structures that are conducive to violence remain in place, violence will be conserved. However, Bourdieu's metaphor also offers us the conceptual possibility of a different kind of outcome. If electricity can be transformed, then what would be the individual, social, political, and economic changes required to transform the structures perpetuating such terrible human suffering toward ends that are peaceful, dignified, and humane?

It is to contribute to such processes of transformation that I have written this book. My initial aim had been to share with global audiences—to "make explicit"—the experiences of young Congolese people so that others might also learn from and be inspired by their strength, courage, and capacities to survive.[12] However, the case study of the DRC also presents empirical evidence on how good-willed international interventions are not adequately responding to the needs of people they claim—indeed exist—to protect. The narratives in this book elucidate some of the individual and social experiences with and impacts of international interventions. They beg reflection on the possibility that such interventions may be contributing to greater

harms in the DRC by obscuring the complexities and rootedness of violence. Such obscuration—clad in aid projects and
donor funding appeals—precludes the clear analyses and effective collective action that would be needed to deconstruct the
systemic inequality and injustice that perpetuate violence in the
DRC and beyond.

I am aware that such a critique is hazardous in an era when
political cynicism is deepening and when populist rhetoric is
increasingly used to mobilize fear and to attribute blame for
adversity and hardship. Providing evidence of the failures of
current international protection efforts may risk buttressing the
political proponents of harsher and more insular policies. Yet, as
taught by the eighth-century Buddhist scholar Shantideva, ours
is an interdependent existence—any of the most pressing issues
facing our world today serve as testimony to this old wisdom. It
is increasingly undeniable that sooner or later we will face the
consequences of our actions and nonactions in perpetuating or
transforming violence.

Rather than pandering to cynical interests, this book is
intended as an offering to honest debate and critical reflection
among the researchers, students, practitioners, and policy makers
who are concerned with—and in many cases devoting their lives
to—redressing the global injustices of our times. In anticipation
of possible frustration among readers, I disclaim from the outset
that this book does not offer solutions to end violence in the DRC.
As the following chapters will show, the DRC has been the "beneficiary" of many decades of exogenously imposed "solutions."
Based on my experience, the inefficacy of international protection
responses is at least in part due to the implementation of simple
and technical responses that insufficiently account for, or even
understand, the historical depths of violence, its pervasiveness

throughout Congolese society, and its intimate linkage and interdependence with the global economic and political system.

As the narratives presented here will show, current approaches to addressing violence in the DRC are not working or at least are not producing the necessary positive results commensurate to the energy and resources expended. In some cases, they are leading to negative distortionary effects; for just two examples: the global outcry about militarized sexual violence has led to a warping of the Congolese justice system and the valorization of women as victims, while the international ban on conflict minerals has also led to unintended consequences, increasing hardships for the artisanal miners digging for their daily survival.[13] At the other end of the spectrum are the massive global development processes that aspire to lofty ideals and the achievement of measurable targets, yet which—despite the billions of dollars invested in them each year—have changed very little, if anything, in the daily lives of the vast majority of the Congolese population.

It is also important to note that this book is not intended as an academic text. While it builds on my doctoral dissertation and years of applied research, my aim has been to make it accessible to a broad audience. This is in line with the mission of the California Series in Public Anthropology, which is to increase understanding and knowledge of major public issues.[14] For readers interested in the theoretical foundations on which this book has been based, or for deeper knowledge about the DRC, references are clearly indicated in the endnotes and bibliography.

This book is my personal story, and I share it with the hope that it may contribute to the efforts of the many thousands of highly committed and caring protection actors toiling to redress the dysfunctions and injustices of the world, giving them the space to pause and to reflect. By questioning the benevolent assumptions and self-evident truths that shroud existing international aid approaches, protection actors may be encouraged to probe the jarring dissonance that exists in the spaces between proclaimed universal rights and the lived experiences of so many hundreds of millions of people today. Renewed reflexive attention on the concept of "do no harm" can support a critical examination of how protection efforts might be inadvertently obscuring the global structures that perpetuate violence.[15] Such reflection might also illuminate the functions that such obscuration may serve.[16] It is through such processes of honest questioning that humanitarian energies may become more usefully channeled toward truly transformative ends.

This book is divided into seven chapters that roughly sketch the trajectory of my own journey into the DRC. Chapter 2 begins with an account of my early years working on the issue of children associated with armed groups. The chapter then takes a historical perspective of the founding violence of the Congolese state, and how these structural violences laid the foundations for the continuing militarized conflict in the Kivus today. Expanding upon Bourdieu's law of conservation of violence, the chapter ends by looking at the mechanisms through which violence is conserved, including through politically expedient reliance on identity-based discourses to mobilize fear and hate, themes that will be taken up again later in the book.

The third chapter deepens the exploration of young people's daily lives in the Kivus. Through testimonies of coping and survival, the chapter bears witness to the capacity of young people to endure the unrelenting burden of entrenched poverty and introduces the concept of psychological resilience, considering its relevance in the resource-poor and socially fragmented

Congolese context. It demonstrates how young people have little choice but to submit to violence in the hopes of surviving it, and thus yield to continued future violence.

Chapter 4 considers how violence is embodied. It problematizes the international focus on militarized "rape as a weapon of war" and considers the negative impact of such international attention. The discussion then turns to other expressions of sexual violence in the DRC and the negative impacts that accompany the selective addressing of only some manifestations of violence. After considering existing gender relations, and how the international focus on militarized sexual violence contributes to exacerbating existing gender inequalities, the chapter closes with a discussion of how structural violence manifests in the bodies of young girls who have few options for survival other than to engage in transactional sex.

The fifth chapter traces the pathways of survival that many young people in the DRC travel each day. Drawing on the sociological understandings of tactical agency, this chapter examines how traditional, family-based support networks have been so weakened by structural violence as to no longer be able to offer the minimum standards of care for their children. It also offers new perspectives on patronage relationships from the view of the "client," whose portrayal of weakness is a tactical choice that both facilitates survival and reinforces weakness, further conserving the structural violences that are increasingly difficult to escape.

Meanings of violence are explored in chapter 6, which considers how processes of meaning attribution help people to cope with unending violence. The chapter highlights the paradox of how identity-based discourses that fuel the conflict in the Kivus are also psychologically helpful in coping processes. In contrast, despite the generalized conditions of lost hope, this chapter documents the narratives of young mothers and older siblings who reveal how caring for children and younger siblings can reignite aspirations and hope for a better future. This chapter considers the processes through which young people's visions of themselves and their aspirations continue to be defined by violence.

Chapter 7 focuses on international approaches to violence in the DRC. It begins by problematizing international protection interventions, highlighting the dissonance between aspirational international norms and lived experiences of violence in the DRC. It critiques the persisting "aid illusion" in the international humanitarian system and strongly argues that more aid money will not end ongoing violence in the DRC. The discussion turns briefly to the global political economy and how it interacts with and fuels violent conflict in the DRC. The chapter concludes by reflecting on how international aid interventions could be reconceived in ways that might do less harm. It suggests that the focus on "doing good" might be more effectively exercised closer to home, with citizens in the global North engaging their political agency to shift the prevailing paradigms of power and inequality that contribute to the conservation of violence in the DRC and beyond.

# CHAPTER TWO

# Outrages in Congo

## SAVING "INNOCENT": THE CURIOUS CASE OF THE "CHILD SOLDIER"

There is something about the extreme violence and brutality lived on Congolese lands that has long captivated the Western imagination. From the 1990s and through the first decade of the twentieth century, one of the most enthralling narratives about violence in the DRC—as elsewhere on the African continent—was the recruitment of children to armed groups.[1] Media coverage widely portrayed the stolen innocence of and irrational savagery perpetrated by "child soldiers" with AK-47s, as newspapers and journals displayed images of half-starved and drugged eight-year-olds manning checkpoints, evidence of the terrorizing barbarity of the post–Soviet era's "new wars."[2] Even more fascinating were stories about the mystical beliefs and practices of some armed groups that compelled children toward logic-defying engagement with violence; in one interview with journalists during a visit to the DRC in 2009, UNICEF's executive director at the time described her shock: "A fourteen-year-old boy whose name translated from Swahili to Innocent, told me he was forced to commit acts of sexual violence against women.... Another still believed that he was invincible against bullets, a common belief among the Mayi-Mayi traditional armed groups in eastern and central DRC."[3] This kind of testimony fueled conceptions about the diabolic otherness of children associated with armed groups. Such narratives were often deployed within aid organizations' communications strategies to raise funds from donors.

By the time I arrived in Goma in 2006, commonly cited estimates were that since 1996, more than thirty-three thousand children had been recruited to and used by armed groups in the DRC. Over the following years I would work with hundreds of such children and would soon come to know them as anyone but hapless victims or dehumanized perpetrators. Many of these children suffered terribly, somehow managing to survive brutal experiences of forced recruitment, then agonizing periods of frontline battle and associated labor. Much of my own work in the DRC in 2006–7 and again in 2009 involved the monitoring of recruitment cases and advocacy to ensure the release of children from the armed groups, and the investigation of alleged child recruitment to establish command responsibility for eventual punitive measures through the UN Sanctions Committee.[4]

Yet as I became more involved in the lives of young former combatants, the complexity of the child recruitment phenomenon began to reveal itself. I learned about the conditions of hardship that led to their recruitment, the limited choices available to them, and their experience during and after armed group engagement. One young man named Joseph eventually became a key informant of my doctoral research. His personal narrative offered rich insights into how young people navigate the extreme complexity of active conflict, how they deal with its aftermath, and how international programs to support the disarmament, demobilization, and reintegration (DDR) of children had done little to achieve their stated aims to improve demobilized children's life outcomes.

In 1996, Joseph had joined the Alliance of Democratic Forces for the Liberation of Congo–Zaire (AFDL in French)—the main rebel alliance of the First Congo War—when he was just seven years old. He explained the circumstances of his initial recruitment as follows: "In 1996 the war came to [my town]. My family fled to Bukavu, where we stayed for three months. When we returned [home], we didn't know who was in charge, though Mzee [Laurent] Kabila was leading recruitment efforts. I joined the AFDL with all the other boys I grew up with. We were taken to the Plains of Ruzizi and trained for five months in how to use guns. After the training we were given arms and uniforms and started fighting. By the time Mzee Kabila took Kinshasa, my battalion had returned to [the base near the airport]."

While the AFDL rebellion was successful in toppling Mobotu Sese Seko in May 1997, the configurations of the national and regional war soon altered, compelling Joseph to navigate the shifting front lines of an increasingly complex regional war. He continued his narrative:

When the RCD [Rassemblement congolais pour la démocratie] entered Bukavu in 1998, they took over our base and killed all but six of the AFDL officers. The soldiers who remained were forced to carry the bodies, they were then forced to douse [the bodies] in petrol and set them on fire. The soldiers were then shot and killed. Other soldiers who had gone to the police seeking refuge were also shot and killed. Six of us managed to survive and we escaped. Two of us hid with our commander. Two weeks later Bukavu was taken by the RCD, so we began our journey on foot to Goma, where we stayed with the family of our commander. He negotiated for us to be integrated into the RCD.

Notable in Joseph's narration was the admiration and appreciation he maintained for his AFDL commander. In contrast to the dominant international narratives about nefarious commanders who violently manipulated the children under their command, Joseph portrayed his commander as his protector and carer and the man who had saved his life.

Four years later, Joseph experienced what he described as the greatest loss of his life, one that led him to decisive action in a landscape of severely limited choices: "One day I was given some days of leave to visit home. Once there I went to visit my grandfather in the nearby village. When I returned home late that day, I found that the RCD had surrounded my house. They were accusing people of being Mayi-Mayi sympathizers. I saw my father as he was being beaten by the soldiers. He was beaten to death. To take vengeance for my father's death, I decided to leave the RCD and to join the Mayi-Mayi." By 2002, at thirteen years of age and having already served on the front lines of active conflict for almost seven years, Joseph was separated from the Mayi-Mayi group as it entered a demilitarization process negotiated during one of the peace accords—one of a series of DDR processes that would be repeated in various iterations over the following decade. He would benefit from the children's DDR program, which included psychosocial support and education programming that aimed to assist his reintegration into civilian life.

Unfortunately, the war in the Kivus continued, and by 2004 Joseph was again left with few alternatives but to join another Mayi-Mayi group. During the infamous battle for Bukavu in

May 2004, Joseph found himself once more on the front lines battling the RCD. Yet, rather than remembering this gruesome operation with anguish, Joseph recounted his involvement in this particular battle with pride: "I participated in the war in 2004 when the RCD attacked Bukavu. We managed to chase them back into Rwanda." Most crucially for Joseph, by playing a part in the victory against the RCD forces, he had been able to avenge the death of his father. This knowledge helped him to deal with what he considered to be his life's greatest loss and allowed him to maintain a sense of self-worth in subsequent years.

When I first met Joseph in 2010, he was twenty-one years old. He was struggling to earn the money he needed to survive each day. Although he had again been enrolled in a children's DDR program after the 2004 conflict and had once more received "reintegration" training to become a mechanic, he could not find a job. Instead, Joseph was subsisting through daily wage labor, transporting heavy loads from the port up the long climb into town. It was grueling work that might earn him the equivalent of one US dollar per day. As I came to know Joseph better, I would learn that it was not his history as a "former child soldier" that distressed him but his inability to effectively surmount the challenges of daily survival.

Without the capacity to meet his basic needs, Joseph had stopped thinking about any kind of prospect for a more positive future. What surprised me about this was that Joseph had been a full "beneficiary" of two phases of children's DDR programs, yet neither of these programs had made any significant difference in his life in the longer term. While in the first instance, in 2002, it was clear that "reintegration" could not happen due to the persisting conflict, the failure of Joseph's second passage through the children's DDR process required deeper investigation.

When Joseph had entered the second DDR program in 2008, a robust international normative framework had been firmly established to protect children from recruitment into and use by armed groups. As defined by the 2007 Paris Principles—or the Principles and Guidelines on Children Associated with Armed Forces and Armed Groups—a "child soldier" was any person younger than eighteen years of age and included "children, boys and girls, used as fighters, cooks, porters, messengers, spies or for sexual purposes. It does not only refer to a child who is taking or has taken a direct part in hostilities."[5] International law had criminalized the recruitment and use of children, and the Rome Statute that established the International Criminal Court listed it as a war crime: "Conscripting or enlisting children under the age of fifteen years into the national armed forces or using them to participate actively in hostilities."[6]

Children's rights to full DDR support had thus been enshrined in internationally accepted principles, and a generic approach to children's DDR had emerged. At that time, the process was generally organized in three key phases. First, for disarmament, children would be identified among an armed group, usually through monitoring reports by UN observers, NGOs, and other local actors. Child protection actors would usually then engage in advocacy with the armed group commanders to ensure that any children under their command would be released. Once separated, children would be taken to transit care centers to begin the second stage of the process—"demobilization"—which was a transitional period that might last several weeks or many months and usually involved social, psychosocial, educational, and recreational activities conceived to support children's eventual readaptation to civilian life. Once "demobilized," children would be given certificates confirming their status and then returned home, thus beginning the third and last phase of the DDR process: "reintegration." Children would be enrolled in one of a selection of reintegration programs that might include schooling, vocational training, or an income-generating activity.

Over the years of my work in conflict-affected contexts, I repeatedly witnessed the weak conception and poor implementation of children's reintegration programs. The Paris Principles define reintegration as "the process through which children transition into civil society and enter meaningful roles and identities as civilians who are accepted by their families and communities in a context of local and national reconciliation."[7] In practice, the programming support provided to children was consistently unable to meet their reintegration needs.

Such failures were clearly and simply articulated in the narrative of Christian, another young man I worked with closely during my doctoral research. He described how the support he had received from a child protection NGO had done nothing to help him meet his everyday survival needs. He had gone through the children's DDR process in 2006 and enrolled in a skills training program that was designed to help him earn a viable livelihood and return to civilian life. When I met Christian in 2010, he was twenty years old and struggling to survive each day. As he explained:

Before the war, I was a student. I had to stop studying in 2002, after my third year of school. We didn't have any money, and I was responsible for taking care of my brothers. When the war came here, we were displaced to Walungu, where eventually I was taken by the [militia]. I stayed with them until 2006. There was so much suffering in those years, but I was quiet because that's life. Once I got out, I went to [the local child protection NGO] for demobilization and reintegration. They gave me training and they promised me a job. But they lied—I never got a job. I got my [demobilization] certificate, but what good is a piece of paper? I dreamed that at this age I would be doing something different, that I would be able to care for my brothers, but I can't. My parents left during the war. After my father was chased away from our land in Mushinga, he went to Maniema to look for gold, and we haven't heard from him since. My mother is a merchant in the gold mines in Mushinga. She prays for me every day that I may find a job. A job is the most important thing for me.[8]

According to both this young man and Joseph, the clearly elaborated children's DDR framework, and in particular its reintegration aspects, had done little to help them "enter meaningful roles and identities as civilians," despite the DDR program's aspirations. More disconcertingly, several other young people described their situation after having gone through the children's DDR process as more precarious than before. This was especially the case for a group of young women who had been separated from the Forces Armées de la République Démocratique du Congo (FARDC). One young mother who had served with the national army for five years regretted no longer benefiting from the relative security that came with mobilization: "Now that we're out of the army, we're unable to get enough work to support ourselves and our children. Our friends who stayed in the army, at least they receive a salary at the end of the month. They have access to food and protection from their husbands. Military lifestyle was a kind of protection for us."[9]

Over the years I tried to work through why it was that children's DDR programs were consistently inadequate in meeting the reintegration needs of children exiting from armed groups. The clearly elaborated international framework was supported by an arsenal of technical guidance, including family reunification, formal and nonformal education, psychosocial support, and vocational skills training. Yet the gap was vast between technical ideals clearly elaborated in guidance documents and the actual experiences of children and the challenges they faced.

Whenever I asked practitioners for their perspectives on this gap, their explanation pointed to the insufficient donor funding of reintegration programs. According to this logic, if there was more funding, and for longer periods, children's DDR programs would achieve their stated aims. Yet it was also obvious to many practitioners that the underlying socioeconomic conditions in the DRC were so dire in general that the obvious question was: "Reintegration into *what?*" For children were simply being sent back to the situations of impoverishment and family breakdown that had been conducive to their recruitment in the first place. The struggles of Joseph, Christian, and the hundreds of other young former soldiers whom I met over the years were poignant to witness, but regrettably they were not so different from the struggles of countless other young people throughout the DRC who battled ceaselessly with the daily toils of poverty.

What perhaps made the situation more difficult to confront for the young people who had gone through the DDR program were the unrealistic expectations that had been set up for them. For example, the "meaningful roles and identities as civilians" promised by the internationally elaborated DDR program sought to encourage a life for children in an environment of peace and development. Yet in the Kivus, war had become the way of life—the only one known to young people born after 1993—and daily survival was a challenge for most of the population.

A further weakness of the children's DDR approach was that it was highly technical, sequenced primarily as a logistical process that could be generically implemented by international child protection actors. Yet, this approach could not be adapted to the highly nuanced and multidimensional experiences of each child. As political scientist Gérard Prunier had earlier discerned, the complexity and rootedness of the "child soldier" phenomenon in the DRC suggested no simple pathway into or out of armed groups: "Young local boys ... came in droves: massive rural poverty, lack of schooling opportunities, boredom, disgust with Mobutu's decaying rule, all combined to give [Laurent Kabila] in a few months an army of 10,000 to 15,000 *kadogo* ('little ones'). They ranged in age from ten to twenty, with a median age of around fifteen. Many were orphans, their parents having died either from diseases or in the Kivus ethnic wars that had been endemic for the past three years. They looked up to the revolutionary leader as a charismatic father-like figure."[10]

Children's reasons for joining an armed group were highly complex and were contingent upon a wide range of individual life factors, which themselves were in a constant state of flux. While it was well established among practitioners that young people joined armed groups for a wide variety of reasons that included poverty, lack of educational opportunities, unemployment, and loss of family members, the education, skills training, or income-generating projects could not manage to push back the structural forces of poverty and absent services.

Young people clearly articulated how the structures of violence were so overwhelming that all they could do was to discern when mobilization might offer the best possible of a range of poor outcomes. One young man described how he had been recruited to the Mayi-Mayi: "One Sunday—it was either in December 1998 or January 1999—I was in church. The Mayi-Mayi came to recruit us. Before then, I had already considered joining. Life was so difficult, we were forced to transport for the different armed groups, we were beaten by soldiers. There was always so much suffering. I thought that maybe life with the Mayi-Mayi would be better."[11]

In a context of such deeply rooted violence, young people I knew believed that the only way to assert themselves was by taking up arms. As one participant in a group discussion explained: "In this *état de guerre* [state of war] power can only be held by the one who has a weapon."[12] Violence had become internalized in their worldviews as they had known nothing different. As described by one young man in a rural town in South Kivu:

> Since 1994, power has been with the military—their weapons are their power. We will do whatever they ask us to. As youth, we feel powerless, we feel bad. If we go to the fields [to cultivate] we have to have money in our pockets so that we can buy our way out if they stop and threaten us. To cross any checkpoint, we have to pay. We can't even get to Bukavu. This takes away our dignity. We are forced to do things under the threat of guns and knives. Their weapons keep us from moving and prevent us from talking.... People should be given power, but here it's taken from us.[13]

It became increasingly clear to me that if I was to ever effectively support the protection of young people in the DRC, I would have to understand this "common sense" of violence. I would have to dig deeper into history.

FOUNDING VIOLENCE

History tells a grim story about violence on Congolese lands. The vast geographic expanses of the Congo Free State were first etched out during the 1884–85 Berlin Conference, when it came under the personal rule of Belgian King Leopold II. As Adam Hochschild narrates in *King Leopold's Ghost: A Story of Greed, Terror and Heroism in Colonial Africa* (1998), the extremely violent methods of conquest during Leopold's reign were integral to his strategy of territorial domination and control, designed to maximize the exploitation of rubber, ivory, and copper. These foundations of violent, extractive rule established an approach to governance that continues to this day.[14]

Between 1885 and 1908, an estimated eight to ten million people died as a result of disease, famine, and torture. These atrocities were documented by George Washington Williams, an American journalist who was also a lawyer, minister, and former soldier. Williams had traveled to the Congo in 1890, and what he saw was an outrageous affront to the supposedly humanitarian enterprise that King Leopold II was claiming to lead. In a letter addressed to the king, Williams reports that the Congolese people he met "everywhere complain that their land has been taken from them by force; that the Government is cruel and arbitrary, and declare that they neither love nor respect the Government and its flag. Your Majesty's Government has sequestered their land, burned their towns, stolen their property, enslaved their women and children, and committed other crimes too numerous to mention in detail."[15] Williams goes on to decry the forced labor system, including the subjugation of migrant workers brought from other parts of the continent. He provides a list of abuses that he witnessed firsthand: "Your Majesty's Government is excessively cruel to its prisoners, condemning them, for the slightest offences, to the chain gang, the like of which cannot be seen in any other Government in the civilized or uncivilized world. Often these ox-chains eat into the necks of the prisoners and produce sores about which the flies circle, aggravating the running wound; so the prisoner is constantly worried. These poor creatures are frequently beaten with a dried piece of hippopotamus skin, called a 'chicote,' and usually the blood flows at every stroke when well laid on."[16] Williams recounts slave-hunting raids, razing of villages, maiming of hands, murder, and acts of cannibalism. These grotesque expressions of violence were later documented by many others, including European and American missionaries.

The knowledge of these atrocities eventually reached Europe, spurring activists to mount what some consider the world's first global human rights campaign.[17] As documented in Hochschild's history, men such as Edward Morel and Roger Casement, and the Congo Reform Association they would establish, labored tirelessly to raise awareness among European leaders about the atrocities under way in the Congo Free State. The great writers of the day joined the cause, including Joseph Conrad with *Heart of Darkness*, Mark Twain with *King Leopold's Soliloquy*, and Arthur Conon Doyle with *The Crime of the Congo*.

Although this violence was moderated by the Belgian state when it took over administration of the territory in 1908, the priority on extracting natural resources continued. Great wealth was generated not only from rubber, copper, diamonds, and gold but also from agriculture. Forced migration of laborers fueled the economy and was practiced especially in the eastern regions. In the decades from 1920 until independence, more than a hundred thousand people were brought to the Kivus to labor on the farms and dig in the mines. Additional migration occurred from the neighboring Belgian colony of Ruanda-Urundi—modern-day Rwanda and Burundi—with laborers eventually settling in the territories of Rutshuru and Masisi.[18]

These newly settled "people of Rwanda," also known as Banyarwanda, were Rwandaphones and were administratively designated as "nonnative" Congolese by the colonial authorities. Local populations felt threatened by these newly arriving people. Rwandaphone "foreigners" could not own land and did not fall under the customary systems that had been co-opted by the Native Authorities. Without local protection, the laborers from Ruanda-Urundi found themselves in a precarious position, unprotected by the state and vulnerable to attack. It is these historic beginnings that laid the foundations for the conflicts over land and belonging that continue to reverberate today.

From this early period, possession of land and accordance of citizenship became tightly linked with identity politics, and regularly contested through violence. The first identity-based wars of the postindependence era occurred in 1964 in South Kivu and in 1965 in North Kivu. These conflicts pitted the Rwandaphone population against those who considered themselves autochthons. Uncertainty, fear, and resentment became some of the most effective tools for political and economic manipulation, including by President Mobutu Sese Seko, who would eventually become one of sub-Saharan Africa's most notorious leaders, and one of Western governments' greatest allies. In the Kivus, Mobutu was astute in deploying the threats of contested identity to his political advantage. By fomenting competition over land and decreeing unstable citizenship policies, Mobutu maintained his influence over the restive eastern provinces.

In 1972, Mobutu passed the Citizenship Decree, according citizenship based on identity group presence in Congolese territory before 1960. This reversed the colonial legislation that had designated citizenship based on identity group presence in the territory as of 1885. Subsequently, Mobutu's Bakajika land reforms of 1968–73 led to the passage of the 1973 General Property Law in which all land formerly owned by private Belgian interests was nationalized. This land, primarily in Masisi and Rutshuru territories, was sold to individuals favored by Mobutu, who were at that time mostly Kivu-based elites of Tutsi identity who had previously been excluded from landownership. In this way, Mobutu gained much-needed political loyalty in the Kivu periphery, helping to consolidate his rule over the vast Zairian nation.[19]

By the early 1980s, however, the power balance again shifted. Non-Rwandaphone Zairians who considered themselves the only legitimate owners of the land pressed Mobutu to repeal the citizenship rights of anyone who could not prove their identity group presence in Congo prior to 1885. Without citizenship, land could not be held. This 1981 Citizenship Law excluded a large proportion of the Rwandaphone population settled in the Kivus, which led to a fission in the Banyarwanda population: Rwandaphone Congolese living in the Hauts Plateux of South Kivu declared their Banyamulenge identity (Banyamulenge translating as "people of Mulenge," the hills of the Itombwe, South Kivu), and the Congolese Hutu of Rutshuru distinguished themselves from other Rwandaphones by claiming a longer historical presence in the Kivus.

The identity-based political violence that had simmered in the 1960s and 1970s worsened in the 1980s and 1990s as the process of "democratization" imposed on Mobutu by Western governments gained momentum. The Conférence Nationale Souveraine, or Sovereign National Conference, convened by Mobutu in 1991–92, provided a forum for further mobilization and division along ethnic lines, rallying autochthonous Congolese against "Rwandan foreigners." To distract his opponents and divide any credible opposition, Mobutu increasingly relied on identity-based political strategies.[20]

Interethnic violence was particularly virulent in the Kivus, where fears of the demographic strength of Banyarwandans led other ethnic groups to mobilize along identity lines. Particularly concerned with the democratic weight of the large Hutu population in the planned 1993 local elections, the North Kivu governor encouraged ethnic Hunde and Nyanga youth militia to kill Banyarwanda Hutu in Walikale, Rutshuru, and Masisi. Up to 10,000 people were killed during this phase of the conflict, and an estimated 250,000 others were displaced in North Kivu.

## MILITARIZED VIOLENCE

It was into this highly charged conflict dynamic that, in the wake of the 1994 Rwandan genocide, an estimated one million Rwandan Hutu refugees arrived in the Kivus. Although contemporary narratives of conflict in the Kivus often begin with the 1994 Rwandan genocide, the genocide only fed into an already tense and specifically Congolese political situation in which identity-based politics had long served as a powerful tool for further mobilization to violence.[21] Prior to the genocide, approximately half of the four million people living in North Kivu were of Banyarwandan descent, with most of the Hutu population living in the territories of Masisi and Rutshuru. With the arrival of the Rwandan Hutu refugees, the tenuous ethnic balance in the Kivus was further destabilized.

Among the refugees arriving in eastern DRC were approximately thirty to forty thousand elements of the former Forces Armées Rwandaises (FAR) and Interahamwe militia responsible for carrying out the genocide. Importing their Hutu-power ideology from Rwanda, they were able to gather local support for their attacks against the Congolese Tutsi population living in

Rutshuru and Masisi territories. The ex-FAR reorganized itself first as the Armée de Liberation du Rwanda (ALiR) and then as the Forces démocratiques de libération du Rwanda (FDLR), which would become the most entrenched of all rebel groups operating in eastern DRC.[22]

The resource-rich provinces of North and South Kivu consequently became the launching grounds in 1996 for "Africa's World War," which was effectively two consecutive wars that drew in nine countries and lasted for seven years.[23] At the culmination of the first war (1996–97), the Forces Armées Zairoises (FAZ) of Mobutu Sese Seko fell to the Alliance des Forces Démocratiques pour la Libération du Congo (AFDL), which was led by Laurent Desirée Kabila. Kabila, a long-term revolutionary known to have met with Ernesto "Che" Guevara in Tanzania in 1965, would take over the Congolese presidency. In 2001, Laurent Kabila was assassinated, then succeeded by his son Joseph Kabila, who remained in control throughout the period covered in this book.

The Second Congo War (1998–2003) resulted in an effective split of the country, with the eastern provinces, including the Kivus, coming under the control of the Rassemblement Congolais pour la Démocratie (RCD), essentially a proxy government for Rwanda. At the local level, Congolese Mayi-Mayi forces mobilized to protect local interests and to gain control of land and resources. Initially a product of the 1960s autonomy movements, Mayi-Mayi groups resurged during the 1996–2003 wars. Usually monoethnic, their political claims formed along identity-based lines, and their discourse generally decried the presence of foreigners, in particular Tutsi Rwandaphones.

International UN peacekeepers arrived in 1999, establishing the Mission de l'Organisation des Nations Unies en République démocratique du Congo (MONUC), which would become the largest UN peace operation at the time and would eventually transform into the Mission de l'Organisation des Nations Unies pour la stabilisation en République démocratique du Congo (MONUSCO). By 2003, the national armed forces had been reconfigured into the FARDC through a continuing process of *brassage*, or integration, of the former rebel groups into one national army.

Although formal peace was finally negotiated at a national level in 2003, conflict continued in eastern DRC. The 2006 presidential elections—the first in the DRC since 1960—officially ended the "postconflict transition" period and legitimized Joseph Kabila's leadership, but they resulted in renewed political violence in the Kivus. Military offensives continued in the following years, despite various iterations of Kinshasa-led, UN-supported, and Kigali-influenced negotiations. The Congrès National pour la Défense du Peuple (CNDP), a reconfiguration of the former RCD armed wing, eventually won its military offensive against the DRC government.[24]

The Goma Peace Accords were signed in early 2008, and although the CNDP had been integrated into the national army, fighting continued. A deal brokered between Kigali and Kinshasa at the end of 2008 resulted in joint Rwanda-DRC military operations (called Umoja Wetu, or "our unity" in Kiswahili) aimed at eradicating the FDLR presence in the Kivus. This was soon followed by the FARDC-led, MONUC-supported Kimia ("quiet") II operations, marking a fundamental shift in the politico-military balance that had held since the end of the Second Congo War. Until that time, the FDLR had largely coexisted with the DRC government and the local population. The FDLR's presence had often been instrumentalized to the advantage of national and regional political entrepreneurs.[25]

In direct response to the 2009 offensive, the FDLR conducted ravaging reprisals on the civilian population. The humanitarian consequences of these attacks were devastating, and the investigation of grave human rights abuses constituted much of my work in the DRC during that year.[26] From the beginning of the operations in January until September 2009, Human Rights Watch documented the killing of more than fourteen hundred civilians, more than seventy-five hundred cases of sexual violence against women and girls, and the forced displacement of more than nine hundred thousand people.[27] The FARDC also conducted attacks on the civilian population, including Hutu refugees who lived in proximity to the FDLR.

While international and regional attention remained focused on routing the FDLR in the following years, by 2012 conflict resurged, as several key CNDP leaders created the new Mouvement du 23 mars (M23) group, justifying their rebellion with the same discourses as in the past.[28] Following sustained fighting with the FARDC, the M23 occupied Goma in November 2012. International outcry, including about the lack of defense by the UN peacekeeping mission, led to a strong and eventually effective military response to push back the M23. A cease-fire and a new series of peace talks led to the disbanding of the M23 in November 2013. Attention could again turn back on the FDLR, and in 2014 a voluntary FDLR disarmament process was organized. It ultimately failed, and renewed military offensives began in January 2015. Called "Sukola II" ("clean up" in Lingala), this operation was unilaterally conducted by the FARDC as the UN had blacklisted several of the FARDC commanders for allegations of previous human rights abuses and thus could not offer its support to the government forces.

Since my last visit to the DRC in 2016, the various iterations of militarized violence in eastern DRC have continued.[29] As this book went to press, tensions in the DRC were high because of the repeated delays in presidential elections that should have been held in 2016 but still had not occurred; popular protests had been violently repressed, and renewed fighting threatened ahead of the promised elections in December 2018. The "common sense" of militarized violence that has guided Congolese politics throughout the DRC's history continues to prevail.[30]

## CONSERVING VIOLENCE

The historic violence that lays the foundations for contemporary violence in the DRC offers the perfect case study for Bourdieu's law of conservation of violence.[31] The mechanisms for this conservation are evident in identity-based distrust and fear, regularly articulated through victim-perpetrator discourses and blame on the "other" for experiences of loss and hardship. By linking identity to survival, the use of violence is justified and perpetuated. In  the Kivus, as elsewhere in the DRC, the tone of identity-based discourses rises and falls in accordance with perennially shifting political and military configurations. The resulting fear, hatred, and distrust are nurtured, feed back on each other, and are transmitted to subsequent generations.

The process through which young people incorporate such narratives of violence was explained to me by a local administrator: "[This town] has been the central theater of so much of the violence in South Kivu. Conflicts over land are old here—the conflicts are between communities and between the various ethnic groups. Young people learn from adults and then assume the same perspectives. Today young people won't know the

difference between Hutu or Tutsi, they just hear the Kinyar-
wandan language spoken and know immediately that these are
people who are competing with them for their land."[32] The
potent interconnectedness of identity-based discourses and
the politics of landownership in the Kivus contribute to the
intractability of political violence there. The two dominant and
irreconcilable narratives are historically rooted and remain
deeply entrenched: either the "autochthonous" Congolese have
had their land appropriated by the "foreign" Tutsi and Hutu
aggressors, or the Rwandaphone Congolese have been denied
access to their own land or protection from the state.

The 1994 Rwandan genocide was the key narrative used to
justify the need for militarized protection, as was reinforced by
multiple episodes of violence against Rwandaphones in the
Kivus over the last decades. Among many non-Rwandaphone
people in the Kivus, blame for the violence and adversity experienced is directly attributable to Rwanda. In 2009, I traveled to
Kasika, a small village in South Kivu, to investigate allegations
that a local Mayi-Mayi group was actively collaborating with
the FDLR. Coincidentally, the day of my visit to Kasika marked
the ten-year commemoration of the 1999 Kasika massacre, where
1,041 civilians had been allegedly killed during an RCD offensive during the Second Congo War. The people with whom I
spoke offered detailed narratives of the gruesome events they
had survived. They had witnessed the rape and killing of nuns,
the cutting open of pregnant women's torsos and the removal of
their fetuses, the clubbing to death of anyone unable to run
away, or their swift decapitation.

When I asked my interlocutors to help me make sense of this
extreme and disproportionate use of violence against the civilian
population, their answers were unequivocal: the humiliation of

having lost a senior commander during a local Mayi-Mayi attack was to be punished. According to them, the brutality of these attacks was meant to serve as a warning to teach the local population to fear the power and strength of the RCD and Rwandan forces. For the survivors of the Kasika massacre, the humiliation of the violence experienced in 1999 resurfaced in 2009, when the operations against the FDLR were launched. The bitter irony for the people of Kasika was that the 2009 FARDC deployment to their area was led by the same commanders who, formerly associated with the RCD and now integrated into the national army, had perpetrated the 1999 massacre. For them, the DRC government's decision to deploy the same commanders to Kasika served as a confirmation of their powerlessness, a reminder of all they had to fear.

Fear and distrust have been assimilated by young people whose social memories have been transmitted to them by earlier generations. As described by one young person in Bukavu: "They came with their military and bullets to benefit from the wealth of Congo.... The war remains fixed in our memory. It started when Rwanda entered the Congo. Before then, Congo was good—or at least that's what our grandparents tell us.... Now, since the Hutus came there are military and bullets. It was the first time we'd ever heard gunfire. We didn't know why they'd come, just that they were here. The Rwandans are our true enemies."[33] Another group of young people in a rural town in South Kivu recounted the beginning of the war as they had heard it described to them. As one young person for that group recalled: "The conflict started when the Hutu entered Congo, they spread throughout all the forests in Congo. We helped them, but soon they turned to pillage and rape and abduction.... There were many barriers, so many taxes to pay.

We were forced to transport goods for the Hutu. We carried large loads for them."[34]

Young people explained the origins of the ongoing fighting in the Kivus in ways that blurred a pragmatic analysis of contestation over land for control of wealth with an identity-based perspective: "The conflict here is about land.... The war is being fought for the creation of a Tutsi empire."[35] In contrast, one fourteen-year-old CNDP former soldier explained his reasons for having voluntarily enlisted to advance the "Cause": "I wanted to fight to serve the Cause. We [Tutsi Congolese] have always been attacked by the others. My parents are still living in the refugee camps in Rwanda with fifty thousand of our brothers and sisters. They are suffering there, and even though they want to come back, they cannot as their land has been taken and they fear they'll be killed. I'd like to continue to support the Cause, to protect our people, to make it safe enough for my parents to come back home."[36]

By conceiving of "Rwandans-as-perpetrators," young people would attribute meaning to a situation in which they remained trapped: "From 1995, the Rwandaphones became our enemy, mostly the Tutsi. The RCD controlled the route from Bukavu, they would mistreat all youth, arrest us, search our bodies for signs of being Mayi-Mayi, like tattoos. Young people were forced to join them—anyway youth had no other choice beyond the army. Girls were raped, boys were forced to rape girls, even their sisters. From that time onward, our advancement has been prevented."[37] Another young person held the opposing militia responsible: "Life here is very mediocre because of the FDLR. I was very young during the worst of the war, but I know the FDLR killed people. They beat people, burned villages, raped women. They are of bad heart. They would force children to rape their mothers and those children have had to live with that shame for their whole lives. They'd put babies in the place where they make manioc flour and grind them into nothing."[38] Blame on identity-based "others" has helped young people to make sense of their own lack of progress. As one young person explained, repeating a phrase I heard repeatedly over the years: "The war has made me go backward—today I should be somewhere else in my life."[39] Fear and distrust thus helped young people to cope with otherwise overwhelming conditions that they felt unable to change.

# CHAPTER THREE

# Surviving Violence

## "THAT'S HOW IT IS"

Variations on themes of brutality, the suffering inflicted by political violence in the Kivus is part of the texture of every day. Yet the young people I knew in the Kivus consistently proved themselves far more able to cope with this violence than outsiders might assume. Eric is one such remarkable person. A warm and generous spirit, Eric was twenty-two years old when we first met, and he would become one of my key research participants. His biographical narrative spanned the worst of the First and Second Congo Wars:

> I'm the third child of my family. My mother was killed in 2004, my father in 1997. My father used to work at the Kavumu airport [near Bukavu] as a pilot. At the start of the war, soldiers from the FAZ [Forces Armées Zairoises] tried to force him to fly a plane from Bukavu to Kisangani; he told the soldiers it wouldn't be possible, that the plane wasn't in good enough condition to fly. Then the Tutsi soldiers [AFDL] arrived at the airport and they took him hostage. We didn't see him again.

We stayed only with our mother then. During the RCD war [2004], Tutsi soldiers came to our house, accused us of having worked for Mobutu, of hiding Hutus in our home. They demanded money from my mother. She said we had none, but she gave them our sewing machine. They locked us [the children] into one of the rooms. They were going to rape my mother. We heard her screaming. I was the oldest boy. I forced the door open and saw my mother on the floor. The soldiers told me they'd kill me. One of them hit me. I spat on him. Then they forced me to go with them into the forest.

They gave me a weapon and then taught me how to use it. In the forest, we fought against the Interahamwe [FDLR]. There was a lot of gunfire. Then there was a cease-fire.

We walked to Shabunda. For one week we walked. We didn't eat anything except *ugali* [cassava-based paste]. I was so hungry, I asked a soldier about getting food. He replied: "Do you see any one of us eating meat? Are you so hungry?" He took his knife and held my arm. He cut off the flesh from my arm. He made me grill my flesh, and then he forced me to eat it. I pretended to, but I couldn't. I spat it out when he wasn't looking.

Then there was more fighting against the Interahamwe. I got shot in the leg in a few places and lost consciousness. I woke up later in the hospital in Bukavu. They told me I had been brought there by the ICRC [International Committee of the Red Cross]. I was in the hospital for a month.

One day, people I knew from church found me. They told my sisters where I was, and the next day my sisters came to find me. How they cried. I had left my mother when she was still alive....

[He fell silent and looked down at his hands folded in his lap. After a few moments, he continued.]

That's how it is.

While the details of the violence that Eric described in his biographical narrative rarely emerged in our subsequent discussions, his experience of violence was incorporated in his physical self, his conception of the world, and his way of being in it.

The bullet wounds in his leg had healed badly and continued to cause him significant pain, and the wide, smooth scar running down the length of his forearm served as a visible reminder of what he had lived through while serving for the RCD forces.

Despite the extreme violence he had survived and the terrible burden of trying to cope with the present constraints of poverty, Eric maintained a positive disposition and a seemingly boundless capacity to go on despite it all. This was in direct opposition to the assumptions regarding trauma that were the basis of much of the research and child protection practice at the time that I met Eric. Trauma studies had gained prominence in Western psychology in the 1980s, especially in relation to post-traumatic stress disorder (PTSD). While initially the PTSD diagnosis applied only to American veterans of the Vietnam War, it was soon widely applied across war-affected populations and came to be associated with any "traumatic event that entailed at least the perception of life-threatening danger beyond one's control."[1] Clinically, PTSD is defined as "an anxiety disorder caused by the major personal stress of a serious or frightening event, such as an injury, assault, rape, or exposure to warfare or a disaster involving many casualties. The reaction may be immediate or delayed for months. The sufferer experiences the persistent recurrence of images or memories of the event, together with nightmares, insomnia, a sense of isolation, guilt, irritability, and loss of concentration. Emotions may be deadened or depression may develop."[2] According to the American Psychiatric Association, the criteria for a PTSD diagnosis include a stressor that would evoke significant symptoms of distress in almost anyone; reexperiencing trauma through memories, dreams, or flashbacks; withdrawal from the external world, disinterest, and detachment; hyperalertness and sleep disturbance; guilt about surviving; memory impairment or trouble concentrating; and avoidance of activities that arouse recollection or resemble the traumatic event.[3]

By the 1990s, research into the impact of violent conflict on children drew heavily on this trauma perspective. Psychologists studying contexts of protracted violence such as Palestine and Israel or Northern Ireland hypothesized that extended exposure to conflict would lead to significantly negative impacts on children.[4] According to theorists, "Repeated and chronic stresses may lead to anger, despair, and severe psychic numbing.... Permanent developmental damage is more likely to occur when multiple risks are present in a child's environment and when stressful settings endure as a feature of the child's life."[5] These studies assumed that children exposed to "political violence are more likely to develop a variety of difficulties, including mental health disorders, behavior problems, sleep disturbances, somatic complaints, and altered levels of cognitive functioning and moral reasoning."[6] Children were presumed to experience trauma if they had been victims of any violent act, had lost someone close to them, or had witnessed acts of violence.

This comprehensive application of the notion of trauma began to receive closer examination as researchers came to question its conceptual relevance in non-Western contexts. Critique of the general tendency to pathologize people's experience of war also began to emerge:

> There is no empirical basis for reductionist medicalization that assigns a sick role on such a large scale and indiscriminate basis. The reframing of the understandable distress and suffering of war as a pathological disorder is a serious distortion and does not serve the interests of the vast majority of survivors, for whom posttraumatic stress is more metaphor than meaningful entity. Most

*Western perspective on mental disorders* ⚡

wars are in non-western settings, and the globalization of western psychological concepts and practices risks perpetuating the colonial status of the non-western mind. Every culture has its own frameworks for mental health, and norms for help-seeking at times of crisis.[7]

By the 2010s, child protection approaches in conflict zones began to expand their focus from one on vulnerabilities and weaknesses to also consider children's assets and capacities to cope with conflict.[8] As demonstrated by individuals like Eric, most young people in the Kivus did not outwardly express the trauma symptoms defined by Western psychological theory despite having experienced profound loss, destruction, fear, and uncertainty. Rather than expressing "severe psychic numbing" or "altered levels of cognitive functioning and moral reasoning," the great majority of young people were managing to cope with the extreme adversities and violence with remarkable grace.[9]

### RESILIENCE TO VIOLENCE?

To try to understand how young people like Eric and the countless others I met over the years managed to continue to cope with adversity, I turned to the psychological literature on resilience.[10] This field of study emerged in the 1960s, as researchers examined links between stressful life events experienced by children and the consequent development of mental or physical illness. For example, researchers tried to understand why most children whose parents struggled with mental illness or alcohol addiction did not develop some degree of psychopathology themselves. Initially researchers classified these children as "invulnerable" to hardship, but notions of invulnerability were eventually discarded as further studies showed that children were vulnerable to risk, but that their responses differed significantly depending on variations in individual, relational, and environmental factors. Key protective factors were found to include an individual's personal temperament, the existence of supportive social relations, and the availability of community resources.

The concept of psychological resilience thus gained traction and came to be defined as "a relatively good outcome despite the experience of situations that have been shown to carry a major risk for the development of psychopathology."[11] Early resilience studies focused mainly on children growing up at the margins of Western European or North American society, where the risks they faced were exceptional when compared with those faced by most of the population. Researchers studied the effects of poverty and other social and economic risks on children, as well as the impacts of parental psychological disorders, drug addiction, and alcohol dependence. Studies with "high-risk" children—or those who experience multiple risks such as chronic poverty, parents with little formal education, and disorganized family environments—found that in some cases the experience of multiple risks could even lead to "steeling" effects that strengthened a child's capacity to cope with adversity. Children's capacity for resilience was also found to relate to and impact upon previous and subsequent experiences of risk.

By the mid-1990s, psychologists increasingly applied a resilience framework to studying the impact of protracted violent conflict on children. Results from studies in Palestine and Israel, Northern Ireland, and South Africa showed that children not only were *not* traumatized by their experiences of conflict but generally were able to adapt to and cope quite well with the daily risks and adversities associated with political violence. According to these studies, only a small minority of children growing up during war expressed any form of mental pathology or long-term emotional reactions. Rather than viewing resilience as an extraordinary capacity, researchers began to consider it a common coping capacity that "arises from the normative functions of human adaptational systems."[12]

More recently, resilience research has benefited from the work of developmental psychology, building on the early work of Urie Bronfenbrenner in his book *Ecology of Human Development* (1979). This expanded approach to resilience considers how the "micro" interacts with the "meso" and "macro" levels of society, in continuous and reciprocal processes of feedback. In this approach to resilience, Michael Ungar of the Canada-based Resilience Research Centre defines resilience as "both the capacity of individuals to navigate their way to the psychological, social, cultural, and physical resources that sustain their well-being, and their capacity individually and collectively to negotiate for these resources to be provided and experienced in culturally meaningful ways."[13]

This interpretation of resilience allows for a nuanced appreciation of the many factors that affect well-being in a wide range of contexts. It also offers the space for considering that resilience will express itself very differently depending on the context and the resources that are available in that context. It became clear to me that the concept of resilience in the DRC—if it applied at all—would be different than that understood by Western psychology. Resilience to violence turned out to be a less helpful concept for understanding young people's capacities for coping than I had initially anticipated.

I began to examine how the lack of health-sustaining resources and the constant uncertainty created by ongoing violence interacted with young people's capacities for coping. In the challenging context of eastern DRC, well-being is a highly relative and usually elusive notion; one of the key strategies for coping with violence was submitting to it, yielding to circumstances that were anything but sustaining of well-being. Most of the young people I knew in the DRC were fully occupied in negotiating the best possible outcomes for each day, striving to gain access to any resources available to them, never very far from the edge of survival. It was this daily struggle that most threatened their sense of well-being.

## "c'est penible"

While most research on violence in the Kivus tends to focus on militarized political violence, political violence represents only part of young people's experience. According to the young people who participated in my doctoral research, "violence is everywhere."[14] They easily identified the multitude of violences that affected them each day: insecurity, assassinations, rape, and theft were only the first mentioned in their long list. And they continued, almost without end: injustice and impunity, unemployment, hunger, poverty, sickness, children not being able to afford school fees, and on they would go.

These forms of structural violence were described by peace researcher Johan Galtung as that violence which "does not show."[15] Yet for young Congolese people, structural violence is anything but invisible—it is a central aspect of their everyday experience. The structural violence defining their everyday is palpable, constraining, and suffocating. The conditions of poverty in all its forms—the lack of jobs, the inability to pay school fees, the absence of medical care or the impossibility of being able to pay for it, the lack of clean water or functioning sanitation, the authorities at all levels who use their positions of power to extort whatever resources they can, and the incapacity of their parents to provide the material and emotional support that young people need—are observable and inescapable. These structural violences define their perspectives and prevent them from realizing their aspirations. Young people regularly lamented their inability to escape to a better life, too closed in by the structures of violence that defined for them "this dead Congo."[16]

Pervasive structural violence contributes to a situation in which young people are aware of the limitations prescribing their lives yet are unable to do anything about them. Young people reported having the hardest time coping with the structural violence of the everyday, the conditions of poverty that make their daily survival so difficult, the lack of opportunities to find a dignified means of earning a livelihood, and the bleak horizons of a future that would only offer much of the same suffering, if not worse.

Structural violence permeates and controls so many aspects of young people's lives. As Paul Farmer has described in other contexts, the ways in which "inequality is structured and legitimated over time" is strikingly evident in the DRC.[17] This inability to escape was brought to life to me by Safia, one of my key research participants in a rural town of South Kivu. She was sixteen years old when I met her, and the mother of a six-month-old girl:

> I'm the youngest child of my mother. She died soon after I was born. My father is extremely ill, he can't take care of me. After my mother died, his second wife never accepted me. Now I live in my older brother's house. I don't get along well with my sister-in-law, but I must stay there with them. My brother is also chronically ill;

he can't use his hand and can't work, but we have no means of paying for him to go to the hospital in Bukavu.

Every day we work, *c'est penible* [it's so hard]. I go to the field with
my sister-in-law, we cultivate cassava and peanuts. Every day we
must make the choice: Do we eat what we've cultivated, or do we
sell it? It's never enough for both and we must choose. Each day the
decision is difficult.[18]

During a visit to her home one afternoon, I witnessed the
deep poverty in which Safia and her family lived. The abject
conditions were among the worst I had seen in a rural Congolese
setting. In the spaces between the small huts of their parcel, several older women were preparing food for a large group of young
children. Safia's sister-in-law was extremely thin, with bright red
eyes that reflected chronic illness, and little interest in my presence. Safia's older brother, who was responsible for the survival of
everyone there, seemed comparatively happier to see me.

During our conversation, Safia's brother described his great
frustration with the physical ailment that had debilitated his left
arm and made any physical labor extremely difficult. He showed
me a paper he had received that morning from the local chief: it
was a convocation demanding that he present himself to the
local authorities for having missed the previous day's communal
labor effort, called *salongo* in Kiswahili. When he would eventually respond to this convocation, he knew he would inevitably
have to pay a fine because refusing to do so would only lead
to even bigger problems with the authorities. The tiny amount
of money the family had been working to save for him to go
to the hospital in Bukavu would instead be paid to the local
administrator.

Despite—or perhaps more likely because of—the grueling
inescapability of each day, Safia imagined a very different kind

of life for herself in the future. Among her dreams was to one day become a woman selling fish in the market, a dream that would allow her to avoid the physical exhaustion of cultivation. Working in the market would also reduce the daily insecurity that plagued her walks through the hills to the fields. Safia had been raped by an unknown man on her way home in 2009, and her daughter had been conceived from that rape. Safia continued to feel at risk of attack each day.

In her vision of the future, after establishing herself as a market woman, Safia dreamed of getting married and establishing a stable home. But above all, she affirmed, "I want to be able to take care of my daughter." Safia remained pragmatic; she knew that having been raped, and having chosen to keep her child, dramatically reduced her chances of being considered a desirable wife.

Before leaving South Kivu in 2010, I gave Safia a small amount of money to help her start her fish trade. During a return visit to her town the following year, we discussed her business venture experience. She recounted how her fish trade had started well and had initially been successful. Within a few months, however, her brother had experienced another health crisis. This time, he was rushed to the hospital in Bukavu with the money that Safia provided by selling off her fish. Her business ended, and she had returned to her daily work in the fields.

Safia's brother's condition eventually stabilized, and the gratitude felt by him and his wife elevated Safia within the family's esteem. However, her daughter still battled repeated bouts of severe malaria and typhoid. Consequently, Safia became heavily indebted once again to cover her daughter's medical fees. Given the depth of poverty from which she could not escape, and the poor health of her child and brother, Safia had lost her hope for a better kind of life.

## SUBMISSION TO VIOLENCE

The sense of hopelessness that is the heritage of such entrenched structural violence colors young people's perspectives for the future. Submission to violence has become a learned mechanism among Congolese people, and often an essential one for survival. Rendered powerless by the structures of violence that have "taken everything from us," many people do not believe their situation will ever change.[19] One young man asked me, without expecting an answer: "This violence, will it ever really end?"[20] Young people described politics in the Kivus as "being locked in an infernal cycle of violence."[21] Such conditions of hopelessness have a profound impact on how young people choose to engage with violence; most have simply submitted themselves to it. As one young woman explained to me: "There isn't anything we can do about it, it just happens like that."[22] On an emotional level, such persistent defeat is heavy to bear: "Inside we are destroyed.... We're losing our morale. We are unable to defend ourselves."[23]

Rather than considering submission to be an expression of weakness and helplessness, young people in the Kivus rely on submission as an actively chosen response, a protective mechanism that they adopt, having learned that resisting violence is likely to be followed by greater violence. Young people in one rural town recounted how previous attempts to protest the daily acts of extortion by police and soldiers had led to brutal responses. One young person prefaced an account with a description of the conditions facing women on their way to the market each day to sell their produce, describing how they are persistently subjected to extortion by FARDC soldiers and police officers:

> Women here are taxed at the market every time they go. If a woman arrives with fifty kilograms of produce, like cassava, she'll be taxed by the soldier for at least twenty kilograms of it.
>
> A few days ago, a young man tried to defend an old woman who was being harassed by a soldier trying to tax her at a barrier. The young man was severely beaten by the soldier, and the woman was forced to pay the tax anyway.
>
> This beating reminded us of the time in 2007 when we tried to protest against the police who kept taxing our mothers. One day a police officer took everything from an old woman—all the cassava she was bringing to the market. She had nothing left and was desperate. We decided it was enough, that we had to react. We took that police officer hostage and took his weapon from him. We carried him to the military checkpoint and demanded to get back the cassava that had been taken from our mothers by the police that day.
>
> We got it back, but the next day the police and the soldiers reacted together. They arrested our school prefect. He was tied up and beaten severely. He was dragged along the road throughout the town to serve as a model for us all, and to show the students what happens when we try to stand up to the authorities.
>
> In response, we organized a march and barricaded the road. Even university students from Bukavu came to support us that day. But then the military used their force against us. We were all beaten so severely. Two students died from their injuries.
>
> It was then that we finally realized that power is not ours, that there is nothing we can do to protect ourselves. We are not able to protect our mothers. We learned that anytime we try to defend ourselves, we'll be punished by greater force.[24]

Young people have learned through their own experience the dangers associated with trying to engage with the political structures underlying the violence of each day. Their efforts to stand up to the daily extortion of the police and the military were met with forceful repression, teaching them that the power of violence is greater than that of their will.

Young people rely on tactics of submission to ensure their survival in the short term based on a clear choice calculus. As a young person in Bukavu explained: "They took me by force.... When something like that happens, you have two choices: either you fight, or you run. If you are strong and they are weak, you defend yourself. But if they are in a group, or armed with knives or other weapons, then you run away."[25] Having lived most or all their lives within the structures of violence, young people do not easily imagine any other kind of situation. As explained by a friend in Bunyakiri: "A child born into this has never known anything different, he cannot believe in another kind of reality. For those of us who are older, we knew something different. We have a feeling of nostalgia; we want to revolt. But for the youth, they know no other way."[26]

Young people have learned to fear the use of violence against them and thus do not voice their dissatisfaction with the political situation too loudly. Young people in Bukavu explained why they were afraid of speaking out against the structures of violence through an example of a well-known singer in Goma who had disappeared after having recorded a popular song critiquing the lack of government progress on economic development—the "Cinq Chantiers" were the five pillars of economic development and governance on which President Kabila based his 2006 election campaign and subsequent government strategy: "If we try to liberate ourselves, we'll just be killed. Any protesters are jailed now—like that seventeen-year-old singer who sang against the Cinq Chantiers earlier this year. He disappeared. If we aim to be heroes, we'll be killed like he probably was. So it's better just to suffer."[27]

This fear of dissent was felt not just by young people but also by adults who have a longer perspective. One of my adult informants in North Kivu explained how the culture of fear prevents opposition to the political situation:

> Let's say there are a thousand people who are opposed to what the government is doing. Of them, maybe five of them will refuse to accept the situation any longer. They will rise up. But in rising up, they create great risks for themselves and their families, and they know it. They will be threatened—they might receive a text message, or be told of a rumor about someone threatening to kill them. They might be attacked in their homes. Their wives might be raped. They might be killed.
>
> Maybe a few of them will continue to oppose the government anyway, and they will be attacked. But in any case, they are just the few. The other 995 people will see this—they've seen it all before—and their fears will be reinforced. Because of their fear, they will not rise up, they will not be too vocal in their dissent. They will accept. If we revolt, we'll be killed. Who wants to die? And for what?[28]

While sharing this explanation with me, my friend was visibly angry, yet his anger was superseded by fear and a sense of defeat. Over the years, he had witnessed the killing of outspoken friends and colleagues in Goma and in Bukavu. They had been human rights activists, journalists, and civil society actors whose vocal protests had led to their deaths, but to no change in the situation. As a father of three children and the main income earner for his extended family, survival was more important to him than giving voice to his dissent. He had chosen not to speak out against the profound injustices and imposed fears of each day, knowing that it would be futile to do so. He had internalized this fear and yielded to the powerlessness of his position within the structures of violence. Like the 99.5 percent of the people in his example, he would go on submitting to the political violence that he considered himself powerless to change.

Through their everyday interactions with armed elements—police, military, or those in positions of authority who call on militarized support—young people have learned that they can only yield to the greater power of violence, and that efforts to engage with the system of violence usually lead to greater force being exerted against them. They have learned that submission to violence is the best way to ensure their own protection. Violence thus continues to close in around them.

# CHAPTER FOUR

# Embodying Violence

## PROBLEMATIZING INTERNATIONAL RESPONSES TO RAPE AS A "WEAPON OF WAR"

In the period between 2006 and 2016, militarized sexual violence in the DRC became one of the core issues around which international protection actors mobilized at the global level.[1] Continuing in the tradition of the nineteenth-century human rights advocates who toiled for the end of forced labor in the Congo Free State, London's glistening halls and galleries regularly hosted exhibitions of glossy, blown-up black-and-white photos of Congolese rape victims, faces shadowed and captions italicized, recounting tales of appalling violence barely survived. Ending militarized sexual violence became the rallying cry of European government leaders and Hollywood stars alike, with the DRC usually serving as the campaign's poster child.[2]

When I arrived in the DRC in 2006, one of my first tasks was to support a team documenting grave human rights abuses committed by the FARDC forces during a military operation in a small town in Ituri, a district of northeastern DRC that had experienced horrific violence during the 1999–2003 wars. This particular attack had been led by government troops and had caught the UN off guard as the brigade allegedly responsible for the abuses had recently completed extensive training and received international support. My induction into the world of militarized rape in the DRC presaged the troubling contradictions I would increasingly feel in later years, as I documented in my journal:

[29 March 2006] A constant breeze blew through the tall trees, over the rolling hills. Yet, as one finds in these destroyed places, a sense of stillness prevailed.

We waited silently in a small concrete room, breeze blowing, flies occasionally buzzing. A team of human rights and child protection experts, we had been deployed to this nowhere town to investigate allegations of the gravest of violations against a civilian population—pillage, gang rape, murder—perpetrated by the newly trained and re-formed national armed forces.

Our first witnesses were led in. Three young women hesitantly sat down on the black metal chairs, tie-dyed wraps covering their heads in the hopes of providing them some anonymity as they came to our meeting place. In even voices we introduced ourselves, and our translator explained to the young women why we were there. In turn, they introduced themselves. We could barely hear their soft voices, hands covering their mouths as they were. But we could make out their names and their ages: twenty, nineteen, fifteen.

In the less than one hour that we spent with these three shyly giggling, finger-fidgeting young women, we were told in excruciating and bloody detail exactly what happened on the night of 10 March 2006, when thirty or so elements of the First Integrated Brigade stormed through their town. Our witnesses told us of how, between the hours of 2:00 a.m. and the first strains of sunlight—the "bon matin," they called it—they were repeatedly raped by nine, eleven, twelve men, respectively, each in their respective mud-walled, thatched-roofed houses.

Into silence and stillness they had finally succumbed, and in the bright breezy sunlight of the next morning when the attackers had gone, they tied their wraps and began another day, as they always had.

Was it in fear that they told us their stories? Or in hope?

We took copious notes. We told them of the reports we would write, the advocacy we would committedly undertake on their behalf. And that was the end of our session. Smiling and so quietly saying good-bye, they covered their heads once again and were gone.

As a child protection actor, then human rights investigator in the DRC, I documented the testimonies of hundreds of girls and women who had suffered terrible violence perpetrated by men belonging to all armed groups.

In subsequent years, the DRC would be ingloriously designated "the rape capital of the world."[3] According to Human Rights Watch, writing in 2014: "Horrific levels of rape and other forms of sexual violence have plagued eastern Democratic Republic of Congo for almost two decades. Tens of thousands of women, girls, men, and boys have been raped and otherwise sexually abused. The exact number of victims is unknown."[4]

In contrast, other international actors endeavored to enumerate victims to gain some grasp of the problem. As detailed in the *Report of the Secretary-General on Children and Armed Conflict in the Democratic Republic of the Congo*:

> During the reporting period, widespread sexual violence remained a grave concern countrywide, in particular in provinces affected by armed conflict. The United Nations Population Fund (UNFPA) reported a total of 12,838 cases of sexual violence (against adults and children) in the Kivus and Oriental Province, half of which (6,379)

were allegedly perpetrated by armed elements.... Of this total, 4,572 cases (35.6 per cent) were reportedly committed against children: 1,472 cases in Oriental Province, 2,063 in North Kivu and 1,037 in South Kivu. Among child victims, 13.3 per cent were reportedly younger than the age of 10.[5]

International journalists also attempted to confront the horrors through enumeration. One egregiously violent attack in the territory of Walikale in North Kivu in July and August 2010 was reported in the *New York Times*: "The number [of rapes] reported has grown, to 242 victims from at least 150 concentrated in 13 villages in North Kivu Province, including 28 minors. But ... at least 257 more women had been raped elsewhere in North Kivu and South Kivu Provinces, for a total of at least 499 victims."[6]

This accounting of violence led to an outpouring of internationally funded interventions to support the victims. Projects would include referrals to emergency health services and rudimentary counseling and psychosocial support. Women and girls who could reach assistance programs would be given limited livelihood support to facilitate "reintegration" into their families and communities, as, once raped, survivors would often suffer severe stigmatization and rejection. Sometimes lawyers would be assigned to cases to pursue justice through the strained Congolese courts.

While this assistance did help many victims, other international responses were less innocuous. In the "fight against impunity," international actors pressed for justice and accountability, especially where FARDC commanders were accused of perpetrating the violence. Encouraged by UN staff, funded by UN programs, and supported by UN logistics, "mobile courts" would be set up in remote towns, with magistrates, UN officials, and international journalists helicoptered in to hear witness testimonies, to great media frenzy. Congolese friends and my research participants would at times express their regret about the distortion to the justice system, noting that only if interpersonal conflicts involved accusations of rape might one have a chance at accessing judicial support.

In the years that I worked in the Kivus, internationally funded programs for rape victims burgeoned. By 2009, the Comprehensive Strategy on Combating Sexual Violence in the Democratic Republic of Congo had been elaborated. It included the provision of medical, psychosocial, and reintegration assistance to rape victims, as well as training and technical support to the judicial system. While eventually international protection actors pushed for more holistic responses, the far more prominent trend was to document the largest numbers of victims possible. The larger the caseload of rape victims reported, the greater the likelihood of receiving donor funding. One local NGO director affirmed to me: "We run sexual violence projects because that's what the donors want. We need money to keep our organization going, so of course we'll create projects for girls if that's what donors expect of us."[7]

In the grinding poverty of eastern DRC, international funding has become a key driver of local economies; local actors can thus be understood for seizing such opportunities. Already in 2010, leading scholars Maria Eriksson Baaz and Maria Stern had issued warnings of the increasing "commercialization of rape" in the DRC.[8] As critiqued by Eriksson Baaz and Stern: "In a context of a corrupt judiciary, rampant poverty, decreasing stigma and the almost total absence of basic health and social services, the focus on sexual violence as a *particularly* serious crime and the resources provided *specifically* for survivors of rape give rise to situations where allegations of rape become a survival strategy."[9]

Applied researchers continued their inquiry into the longer-term impact of the international focus on sexual violence in the DRC; in their 2018 article titled "Beyond the Hype? The Response to Sexual Violence in the Democratic Republic of the Congo in 2011 and 2014," Dorothea Hilhorst and Nynke Douma concluded that "the fight against impunity, spearheaded by international actors, has become embedded in the political economy of survival and corruption, and seems to add to moral confusion about gender relations."[10]

Over time, I would also be personally confronted by the damaging impacts of the international spotlight on sexual violence in eastern DRC. Given the proliferation of projects and international support in response to the rape "story line" in the DRC, women and girls soon learned that being a victim of militarized sexual violence would increase their access to services and material benefits provided by international protection actors. Another of my doctoral research participants was Cécile, who was twenty-two years old when I met her. During our first biographical interview, she fluently narrated her story:

> I'd like to tell you the story about my life, even if it's sad. I try to forget things, but it's not easy. I was born of rape. My mother didn't love my father and I didn't even know him. My mother had six children in all. When I was eleven years old, we came to Bukavu. In 2003, during the fighting, I was taken away by the Interahamwe [FDLR]. They took me hostage with another girl, into the forest. It was a Tuesday that day. We were taken to the forest....
>
> It's hard for me to talk about this.... I was a slave for six men, always the same men. I had to do sexual acts for them, it was so difficult. I couldn't eat. It was such suffering.
>
> One day, after two and a half years that I had been with them, they went to a battle. I was left guarded by only one soldier. I asked the soldier if I could go to bathe; he said I could if I had sex with

him first. After I did, I managed to get far enough away from him, and then I escaped. I hid in the forest for two days, I didn't know where I was. Eventually I found the road, and a car stopped to pick me up and took me to Goma.

Once in Goma, I stayed in the market, I went from house to house, begging, living off charity, trying to find work. One day, when I was returning the washing I had done for a family, I was told by the girl living there to wait for her mother to come so that she could pay me. It turned out that her mother was my elder sister.

My sister had thought that I was dead, my whole family had. She cried, how she cried. When I understood it was my sister, I cried too. She had seen me in the market before, but had thought that I was just a crazy woman begging like so many others. I told her it had been my only way to survive. I stayed with her until I returned to my mother in Bukavu.

Eventually I became very sick. I learned I was pregnant. Now I have my five-year-old daughter with me. Like me, she was born of rape.

In 2007, I started at [a local NGO] where I was trained in tailoring. [The same NGO] pays my school fees now. I'm a law student at the university. I dream of becoming a lawyer, to defend women and children. Girls here suffer too much. My role is to be a messenger for all the girls, all the women, all the young people who have suffered like me.

Since 2007, I've traveled four times to speak to officials and leaders. I've been to Nairobi, to Kinshasa, and to Kigali twice. Next week I'll go to Norway to tell my story. My priority now is to advocate for the rights of children born of rape and for those who became mothers against their will.[11]

Cécile is an impressive person; she is intelligent, articulate, and courageous. She had lived through excruciating life experiences, surviving and coping in ways that defied expectations. Having since been provided all the opportunities on offer by the international child protection system—material support, education, training, and even international travel—she had turned her experience into something positive and hoped to use her access to Congolese leaders and international audiences to advocate for the needs of other young people. Cécile was deemed an appropriate target of international protection support and could therefore benefit from unprecedented opportunities. Her education was fully funded, even to the university level, which was an exceptional privilege for any young person in the DRC. Cécile was repeatedly invited to speak at international conferences, opportunities that allowed her to travel and expand her horizons further than most Congolese people could ever even fathom.

Cécile's narrative and the way she projected herself, however, left me questioning whether there might not be negative consequences of all the support she was receiving from the international protection actors soliciting her time. Although she was thriving with all the attention, this attention was based primarily on her status as a rape victim. Through her narrative and the discussions we subsequently had, it was clear that her personal identity was now anchored in her experience of abduction, violence, rape, and unwanted motherhood. At the same time, Cécile's experience was endlessly profiled in the fund-raising efforts of the local and international NGOs that actively promoted her to speak at public events and to meet international donors whenever they visited Bukavu, with funds often awarded as a result.

Far removed from the sophisticated aid machinery of Bukavu, I was nevertheless eventually confronted with the distortionary effects of international responses to sexual violence. In one of the rural towns of South Kivu where I spent significant amounts of time conducting my doctoral field research, I would often enjoy long conversations with Sister Agnès, a Catholic nun who had left the convent during the war to do social service work. Sister Agnès ran a local association that provided shelter to displaced people and connected women who had been raped with medical assistance, food distributions, and psychosocial support projects offered by local and international NGOs.

Sister Agnès often told me about her experiences during the war and of everyday life. With great patience, she helped me to make sense of the historical, contextual, cultural, and gender dynamics specific to that area. Her analyses were always multidimensional and acknowledged the complexity and interconnectedness of it all. When I asked her to describe the phenomenon of militarized sexual violence, she covered themes relating to vengeance, hopelessness, the inability to ensure daily survival, men's psychoemotive need for affection, and their persisting struggle with weakness. She explained how weakness fed into widening and deepening cycles of victimhood, subjugation, shame, and aggression.

One day in 2010, Sister Agnès and I were discussing why there seemed to be a sudden upsurge in rape cases compared with the preceding year. She too had noted a recent increase in her caseload. She was about to go into greater detail about "the 1,820 women rape survivors I have helped since 2002" when she noticed a woman with her young daughter and baby walking toward our shaded hut. She called out and motioned for them to join us. Timidly, the woman approached and, in response to Sister Agnès's insistent urging, sat down with us. Her young daughter leaned into her shyly, while her baby fed quietly at her breast.

The woman held an empty plastic cup, and as she and Sister Agnès spoke with each other, I understood that the woman had come to ask for a cup's worth of flour, something Sister Agnès usually offered to women in need of assistance. Sister Agnès asked me if I would like to hear this woman's story. "Of course I would," I responded, "if she wants to tell it." The woman began her narration, looking directly into my eyes as Sister Agnès translated:

> When the war reached our village, we had to flee. My family and I have lived here by the roadside for several years. We try to get as much food and materials as we can from the NGOs and [the UN World Food Programme], but it's never enough. So usually I go back to our plot of land outside the village to cultivate.
>
> Going to the field is a big risk because in this area there are many armed men who are looking to steal our food. I know the risks, so does my husband. But we have to eat and so I continue to cultivate.
>
> My husband was attacked during the raid of our village that displaced us here. They destroyed his legs and mutilated his penis. He can no longer work in the fields, so he just stays at home. Now it's up to me to find food for us all. Like a little chicken, I will look for food wherever I can. Each day, I either go to our field, or I come here into town to try to find some food.
>
> It's by going to cultivate our plot of land that I've been raped by armed men. In the last years, I've been raped four different times.
>
> You see my daughter here? She's three years old. Last year she was raped too.
>
> The most recent time I was attacked was early this year. I was with my baby. The men took her from me and stuck their gun in her vagina. She was already learning to walk, but since then she's become a baby again. She's one and a half years old, but now it's like she's six months old. Look.

The woman stopped her narration as she pried her baby off her breast. She began to unwrap the cloth that had been tied around her baby's body. When I understood what was happening, I rapidly intervened: "No. Please don't do that. Really. I don't need to see." But the woman and Sister Agnès insisted. The baby began to cry, and I pleaded: "Please, it's not necessary." The baby's cry was loud and piercing now, and her little body flailed in resistance. Sister Agnès, with great authority, placed her hand on my shoulder: "Claudia, it's important that you see this."

There in front of me was the woman's screaming baby, legs opened to display the raw and gaping pink wound of her vagina where the rifle had entered her tiny body. "Do you see?" Sister Agnès asked me. I nodded, silently, and looked down.

Then the mother wrapped her baby up again and placed her back on her breast, soothing her back to sleep. Eventually our conversation ended, and the woman prepared to leave with the cup of flour in her hand. As she turned to walk away, I did what I had years before stopped doing: I reached into my back pocket and pulled out a tightly folded twenty-dollar bill, which I always kept close at hand in case I needed to buy my way out of danger.

Going against my most basic of research principles, I knew even in that moment that I was reinforcing the "pornography of suffering," what Arthur Kleinman has called the "voyeurism" and the "commodification and consumption of trauma."[12] Even though I was giving this money to someone in extreme need, I also knew that my "handout" represented only a momentary respite in her excruciating daily toil. Mostly, I admitted to myself, it was an attempt to absolve myself of all that I could not do, could never undo. It was a futile act to buy myself out of the turgid mix of sadness and helplessness that overwhelmed me in that moment, that stays with me even now, so many years later.

## GENDERING STRUCTURAL VIOLENCE

One of the main weaknesses of international responses to militarized sexual violence in the DRC is that they ignore how generations of political and economic violence have been transposed and incorporated into contemporary Congolese life. To understand how violence becomes embodied in women—and men—the frame of analysis must be wide and deep enough to capture the rootedness of structural violence and the gender-differentiated experience of everyday life.

It was my young research participants in rural South Kivu who most eloquently elucidated this complexity for me when I asked them to analyze the causes of the militarized sexual violence that was at that time the overwhelming preoccupation of so many international protection actors. To my surprise, instead of discussing rape in times of war, they began their explanation by describing the physical extremes that women are subjected to daily and the ongoing battles they wage to support their families.[13] One young man began the discussion:

> Women here are treated like animals, forced to carry out heavy labor. Here it is considered that a woman should not talk, that she has nothing to say. Early marriage is common, as usually a fourteen- or fifteen-year-old girl cannot continue school because her parents no longer have the means to pay her school fees. Anyway, often men don't want a girl who has studied, because they think she is *complexée* [she thinks she is better than others]. Because the dowry is so expensive, men resent their wives and make them work all day, then all night in bed, just to pay off the debt. A man won't marry a woman who doesn't know how to work.[14]

One of my research participants offered a series of drawings to explain the dire situation of Congolese women in rural areas, accompanied by a written account. His drawings are reproduced on the following pages, with translations included in the caption for each image.

This visual rendition of the gendered experiences of everyday violence is a widely accepted account of the specific challenges

Situation of women in rural South Kivu. Scene 1. In this scene, the woman has multiple jobs. First, she is pregnant. She puts the cassava out to dry in the sun. The wood [that she has collected] is outside. The water container is empty. The child is crying out to be held. The house is in poor condition and her husband watches her as she works. *(Woman)*: "At least take the child as you don't help." *(Man)*: "No, I don't want to, its not my job. I'm resting, aah!" *(Child)*: "I'm hungry." The two mice enter the hut. We should help women. We do not train women only for the fields.

Scene 2. The mother goes to the field with two children, a basket, a goat, and in the basket there is a hoe, a machete, and an ax. The mother suffers, and the father stays behind doing nothing. Oh, what a life for this mother. *(Woman)*: "Oh! My God, what have I done in this world. I don't get to rest, one child on my back the other on my chest and my husband is often without work." Here the mother especially suffers due to the early birth of her baby. The mice enter the hut, objects are left outside that the father does not bring inside the hut. *(Man)*: "That idiot left for the field. I'll continue listening to my music." The state should guarantee and respect personal property. Lets build for goods, not for barriers.

Scene 3. *(Woman)*: "Do we work only for the barrier? By the time we arrive at the market, our basket is already destroyed." A police officer imposes the amount of cassava to be given to him. *(Woman)*: "Another barrier? Oh my God, what can be done?" There are multiple barriers which make our mothers suffer, including the police who always detain people, especially those who come from the market. The state should guarantee and respect personal property. Let's build for goods, not for barriers.

Scene 4. *(Woman)*: "Oh! My God what should I do?" She cuts the wood. The children cry because of the rain.... The child cries in the basket. The mother has stopped cultivating and is cutting wood. But when she notices the rain, she will abandon the wood to take the children who are crying. She will attach the goat to the grass, and the other things lay disorganized in the field. It is such suffering. To prepare them psychologically, let's have sympathy for our women.

Scene 5. *(Woman)*: "Children, don't cry, we're almost there." *(Child)*: "When will we have freedom? Oh my God, help me." The woman is a human being like a man, not a donkey. She returns home in the rain. One child around her neck, the other on her chest, the basket full of wood and the goat attached to a cord that she holds.

Scene 6. She is constantly suffering. When her husband arrives he demands that she give him food. The mother gives him the food, but he asks her what food it is while the children fight over the food. *(Woman)*: "Heh! And what did you bring? Your work is only to stay here at home and drink alcohol." *(Man)*: "Hehe! What kind of food is this. I will beat you. You make salad for me." *(Child)*: "Hey, you're taking it from me." You discipline an animal but not a woman who is a human being.

facing women in rural areas. It also demonstrates the specific difficulties facing men. In a 2011 report, "'Before the War, I Was a Man': Men and Masculinities in Eastern DR Congo," Congolese scholar Desirée Lwambo echoes the narratives of my young research participants and laments the international focus on men as perpetrators. Such a focus damages gendered conceptions of masculinity that have already been devastated by decades of violence and war, as "failed," dysfunctional, and violent masculinities become further warped by conflict and poverty.[15] While far from justifying why men rape, both the narratives of my research participants and the grounded analysis of Lwambo embed violence and shame within the ravaged social and economic structures of contemporary Congolese life.

TRANSACTING SURVIVAL

As I further probed the despairing depths of sexual violence in the DRC, I discovered how the abject conditions of social and economic breakdown continued in their embodiment. As young people repeatedly explained to me, the constraints of poverty, lack of livelihood alternatives, and displacement from family land had led many girls to choose transactional sex as the most accessible and reliable way of generating income. Defined as acts of sex in exchange for money, gifts, or favors, "transactional sex" serves as a prevalent coping mechanism for women in contexts of violence where there are few alternatives for earning one's survival.[16] As described during many of my interviews and group discussions, girls will have sex for just 1,000 Congolese francs (equivalent to US$1 at the time), for a meal, or for material goods such as clothes or skin lotion. Transactional sex had become a matter-of-fact way of life for many girls and young

women. As a twenty-four-year-old woman explained, "I sometimes have sex to earn money. How else could I support myself
and my four children?"[17]

Parents I interviewed acknowledged that their daughters
turned to sex work to meet the material needs when parents
were no longer able to do so. One mother elaborated: "We love
our children ... we don't want them to go to the streets. But since
we are unable to care for them, they decide to go themselves."[18]
Another parent, a father who was also a local chief of a Bukavu
neighborhood, explained his sense of powerlessness to protect
and guide his children: "When I try to prevent my fifteen-year-
old daughter from going out, she responds: 'I will go where I can
eat.' I know she is earning money from men, but I am unable to
stop her."[19]

Transactional sex as a coping mechanism has been studied in
other contexts of displacement and political upheaval, where the
extreme difficulty in accessing food and other material goods
and the lack of any other livelihood alternatives lead women to
engage in sex acts to earn their living. Sex in exchange for material goods thus serves as a type of "interpersonal insurance" to
reduce individual vulnerability in precarious economic situations where "formal safety nets are often missing, and insurance
through informal systems of gifts and loans is rarely, if ever,
complete."[20] The prevalence of transactional sex as a coping
mechanism demonstrates a complex nexus of economic, social,
and cultural conditions.

In the cash-based urban economy of the Kivus, young people
noted that "some girls are so poor that sex is the only way that
they can get any money."[21] This phenomenon is also prevalent in
rural areas, as explained by a fourteen-year-old girl in rural
Masisi: "We're ten children in my family. There are nights that

we don't eat. When we're in this situation, I have no choice but to prostitute myself to earn some money. This is how I survive."[22] Parents would admit that their daughters were engaging in sex to support their survival or to buy material goods. While they lamented that they wished this would not happen, they felt helpless to change the situation: "As we are unable to respond to the needs of our daughters, they will find their own means."[23]

For many people in Masisi Territory on the edge of survival, an armed attack on a village, looting of personal property, or a brief period of displacement could lead to collapse into total poverty. Sylvie was an eighteen-year-old living in one of the displaced settlements not far from Kitchanga town in Masisi Territory, an area that had witnessed repeated waves of population displacement due to regular clashes between the CNDP and the FARDC. Sylvie and her family had been displaced several times in recent years, and the economic strain eventually led to her father leaving home. Soon after meeting another man, Sylvie's mother also left home, designating Sylvie as the head of their household: "About five years ago our father left us. Our mother eventually married another man—then she abandoned us too. We were three girls and three boys. It was up to me to take care of my younger brothers and sisters. My brothers joined the army so they could take care of themselves. But I was responsible for the survival of my sisters." At the time, Sylvie was only thirteen years old. Her brothers could work in the mines, serve as porters, or join one of the several armed groups active in the area: at the time, they considered their most viable option to be enrolling in the CNDP, which would earn them at least a limited income, and perhaps offer some modicum of protection for their sisters. For Sylvie and her younger sisters, however, survival options were more limited. They were living in a

displaced settlement far away from their family land and thus
could not cultivate, while the high level of military activities in
Masisi at the time made work as a daily laborer on the farms too
unsafe. Unable to conceive of viable alternatives, Sylvie turned
to transactional sex. As she told me: "From the age of fourteen, I
started going to boys and old men so that I could provide food
for my little sisters. That's how I got pregnant the first time. I
had my first child when I was fourteen and my second one when
I was sixteen years old. I didn't want to have children then, but
life made it happen. The money that I was given by men helped
me so much that I was able to provide food for my sisters and to
pay for our school fees." Initially sex in exchange for money and
food was a temporary survival measure for Sylvie, but once she
realized that she could support herself and her family in this
way, even to the point of paying her sisters' school fees as well as
her own—a notable achievement most Congolese could not
imagine—it became a more permanent lifestyle.

Sylvie was aware of the risks involved in prostitution and
articulately described the difficulties she experienced in this
line of work: "Prostitution isn't easy work. I have to leave my
children with my little sisters, and sometimes when I come
home in the morning they're crying. But if I don't do it, we won't
have enough to eat or to pay our rent. When I spend the night
with a man, he might easily give me US$5, or sometimes he'll
give me absolutely nothing. He might threaten me because he is
a soldier and so I have to return home without anything."

Later in 2010, I was asked by an international NGO to document the needs of girls living in the most marginalized neigh-
borhoods of Goma. Through this research I encountered the
invisible and brutal world of organized sex work. The adolescent
girls I talked with as part of this research described how life had

led them to where they were, most often as the result of poverty and the inability of their families to offer them the most basic care. These girls had soon learned that with each *passage*—or sex act—they could earn up to US$2, a considerable amount of money for most people in the Congo at the time. While this allowed the girls to buy food and pay rent for a place to sleep, they knew they were running very high risks. They not only had to deal with the mistreatment of their *managers* but also were in constant fear of being infected with HIV or other sexually transmitted illnesses. Even worse, according to their narratives, was the fierce physical violence they faced each day. During an extended discussion with a group of seven girls in a local bar one afternoon, I was told about the abuse they regularly confronted:

> Sometimes we're beaten by soldiers; sometimes they rape us. If they find us in the streets, they'll search us for money, touching our whole bodies. If they don't find any, they beat us. Soldiers usually come to the bar late in the night, and the manager puts pressure on us to have sex with them. If we refuse, they take us to a place seventeen kilometers from here, rape us, and leave us there. What else can we do but accept to have sex with them? They make promises, they tell us they'll take us away from here. But it never happens. Besides the beatings, mostly we're afraid of getting diseases from them. But the civilian clients are the worst; they are well dressed, they might look responsible, but they are the most violent. See these scars on my neck? They came from a time when a man took me to his place and tried to make me have oral sex. I didn't want to, and he beat me with so much force.[24]

Another girl continued:

> A month ago, a man promised that he would pay me to have sex with him if we went outside, next to the slaughterhouse across the street. When we got there, he called out to his other friends who were waiting in the darkness. They pushed me into the area where the goats

are killed and started beating me. I was pushed to the ground. I had animal blood all over me. When I resisted, they threatened to hang me from the hook above where the animals are left to be bled. So I was quiet, I accepted all of them. But another friend had an even worse experience. She had a plastic bag forced inside her vagina, and the man set fire to it. We're very afraid of this happening to us.

When I asked the girls what they would do when these types of abuses occurred, they dismissed even the possibility of recourse: "We can't report these abuses. If we go to the police they'll demand at least US$20. If we cry out for help, we're accused that we found what we were looking for. Even telling you these stories won't change anything."[25]

## SELECTIVE OUTRAGE AND OTHER DISTORTIONS

Outside of the DRC, among both policy-making and academic audiences, my critiques of international responses to sexual violence in the DRC were often challenged. Colleagues would argue that progress for Congolese women was being made, impunity was being confronted, the voices of women and girls, who for so long had been subjected to horrific violence, were at last being heard. How could I possibly criticize these advances?[26]

I understood these critiques, but I persisted: the disaggregation of certain kinds of violence against one category of victim cannot tell a complete story. What about all the other forms of violence, rampant yet unseen, unheard, and continuously, insidiously destroying the fabric of so many lives every day in the DRC?

Their challenge was returned: but you must disaggregate to analyze and respond.

Their challenge continued: Are you saying that rape is not a particularly devastating kind of violence?

I was speechless: How could one ever deny the ravaging devastation of rape?

I offered: What if we were to consider the unintended consequences of all this international focus on militarized sexual violence? What might it be doing to the women, men, boys, and girls of the DRC today? What might be the long-term consequences of valorizing weakness and reinforcing victimhood? What might be the impacts on generations of men, who are being further dehumanized? Might all these international actions be doing greater harm to Congolese society?

Silence.

End of presentation.

I would leave those brightly lit conference rooms knowing I had not managed to convince my angry interlocutors.

How might I have said it differently?

# CHAPTER FIVE

# Navigating Violence

## La débrouille

Young people in the Kivus do all they can to navigate the limitations and opportunities presented to them each day, exercising their agency in courageous ways. The narrative of Richard is just one example; nineteen years old when I met him in 2010, Richard stood out among other young people in his small rural town as he was comparatively successful in running his own business, a carpentry workshop. During his biographical interview, Richard recounted how, following the death of his father in 2001, he had become responsible for the survival of his family:

> My father died when I was ten years old. From then I had to ensure our survival. My mother wasn't in good health so I was responsible for us both. After my father died, I dropped out of school because it was no longer possible to pay my school fees. I traveled to the nearby mines in search of gold. The conditions in the gold mines were so demanding and I eventually realized that I'd probably

never find any gold. So then I began selling beer at the mine. With that I was able to make just enough money for us to live with, but the work was so heavy. The following year, I thought I would try to earn more in the cassiterite mines farther away. The conditions there were impossible. It was so hard, and I spent all the money I earned just to buy food each day and to pay for a place to sleep.

I came back home in 2009, then rented some land to cultivate. I'm growing cassava now, and even with the *mosaic* [plant virus] we manage to cultivate enough for eating. Last year I also participated in a carpentry skills training program [offered by a local NGO] and now I get some jobs as a carpenter, making doors mostly and some furniture. This helps me to support my mother, my wife, and our two children.

Richard's capacity to seek new opportunities required the skill of discerning when to end a venture that was proving to be unprofitable. He was committed to ensuring the survival of his ailing mother and eventually to supporting his wife and children. He was managing to do so, despite the arduous constraints imposed by structural poverty.

When I made a return visit to Richard's home in 2011, he was apparently doing even better than the previous year. His carpentry workshop was receiving regular clients, and his family's needs were provided for. Evidently, Richard was facing the constraints of poverty far better than any of his peers. When I asked him what it was that inspired him to work so hard, he described the responsibility he felt toward his family, which kept him constantly in search of the next possible opportunity. With intelligence and adaptability, he managed to support his family and build a relatively viable carpentry business.

Yet despite Richard's constant efforts, the environment in which he lived conscribed any possibility for emerging from the conditions of rural poverty. As he explained, in the highly militarized environment of the Kivus, simply provisioning the wood for his workshop each week came with significant risks; usually he had to pay soldiers, police, or other armed elements a high price to negotiate his safe passage to and from the forest where he would buy the wood.

Richard did everything in his power to ensure that his children received the best possible care and opportunities. But the school fees and medical bills he labored for merely paid for poor-quality education and substandard health care. Despite his greatest efforts, Richard remained trapped within a system that promised little better for the future of his own children.

Richard's capacity for coping with the hardships of rural poverty demonstrates what my young research collaborators would frequently refer to as "intelligence." According to them, successful coping requires the capacity "to live despite it all. We depend on our intelligence. Intelligence is our capacity to know how to exploit our potential and to seize possible opportunities."[1] This requires "the capacity to look for one's livelihood [*chercher la vie*]. We don't cross our arms, we look to others for help.... Intelligence requires the ability to change behaviors ... to think about solutions and to know how to realize them. It's knowing how to use what we've been given.... Intelligence comes from experiencing difficulties. If one isn't hungry, one won't learn intelligence."[2]

The intelligence described by my young research participants is similar to the sociological concept of "agency," defined as one's capacity to act within and influence established social structures and relations. The concept is useful in examining how young people seize opportunities that might become available and reappropriate certain aspects of an otherwise oppressive system in ways that might become useful to them. Agency is crucial in contexts of hardship, as noted by psychologist Albert Bandura: "Unless people believe they can produce desired results and forestall detrimental ones by their actions, they have little incentive to act or to persevere in the face of difficulties."[3] A structural perspective on individual agency is especially relevant when studying contexts of violence, where living conditions are highly adverse and uncertain. In such constrained environments, Michel de Certeau's study of tactical agency—or how we "use, manipulate and divert" predetermined spaces—is especially illuminating.[4] For example, in their ethnographic studies of young people's agency in Mozambique and Liberia, respectively, Alcinda Honwana and Mats Utas elaborate the concept of tactical agency to explain how young people manage to survive and make the most out of situations otherwise conscribed by violent conflict.[5] They show how the exercise of tactical agency depends not only on individual capacities but also on the social environment and the political structures in which people live.

Given the limitations on agency that are imposed by violence and poverty, agency in the DRC can be considered akin to the capacity for *la débrouille*. *La débrouille* is an ubiquitous concept throughout much of Francophone sub-Saharan Africa, understood by all, and generally associated with the idea of material survival and earning a livelihood.[6] The word is derived from the French verb *se débrouiller*, which can be translated as "to find a way," "to make arrangements," or "to use one's own means."[7] *La débrouille* is a function of everyday life that is understood by all, a specific way of coping that has come to dominate discourses on survival in the DRC. It also serves as an epithet to justify the absence of government services and the prevalence of corrupt practices.[8]

*La débrouille*
*"to find a way"*

Describing the Congolese economy of the mid-1980s, Janet MacGaffey explains how *la débrouille* is a necessary aspect of ensuring one's economic survival:

> The extremely low wages, spiralling prices and scarcity of food-stuffs and goods for sale in Zaire's cities indicate a situation near mass starvation, but somehow the majority of people manage to feed, house, clothe themselves and even find considerable amounts of money as necessary. In the official system nothing works as it should and most people find their principle means of livelihood outside wage earning and the regular channels of distribution. They "fend for themselves" (*on se débrouille*) in Zaire's second economy, in a highly organized parallel system of economic activities that is unrecorded in official figures and reports, but which must be taken into account to arrive at any realistic assessment of life in Zaire today.[9]

At the individual level, *la débrouille* serves as a key coping mechanism that is primarily associated with finding a way to meet one's material needs. Given the lack of employment alternatives and difficulties in finding a way to earn a living for the vast majority of people, the capacity for *la débrouille* allows young people to survive and to make the best of extremely challenging circumstances.

Eager to teach me the language of their everyday, some of my young friends coached me in the most apt response to the common casual Kiswahili greeting—*Unaenda wapi?* (Where are you going?). For young people, the response is usually along the lines of *Ninaenda kujidebrouiller* (I'm going to find my way).[10] Young people spend many hours of each day just looking for opportunities to ensure their daily survival; as they explained, one must always be alert as the capacity for *la débrouille* depends both on one's ability to appraise and make use of potential opportunities, and on the possibility that such opportunities might present themselves at any given time.

## WEAKENED SOCIAL SAFETY NETS

Young people are often left to fend for themselves, as traditional social safety nets no longer hold. In particular, the capacities of families to offer support to their children have dramatically declined in recent decades, seriously affected by the conditions of economic adversity, which, in the Kivus, have been exacerbated by continued violence and insecurity. Throughout the DRC, parents have faced increasing difficulties in meeting their children's basic survival needs, a situation that has had a significant impact on the material and emotional support that parents can offer.

One father, who is also a local chief, described his inability to support his family and the consequences this has for him: "If we're going to talk about the difficulties that parents face here, let's start with me. I have eight children, but only one of them has really turned out all right. The others are all just struggling to get through life with so much difficulty. I have no job, my wife does what she can to get food for us.... Here no one respects me.... My family no longer listens to me because I have no means to provide for them."[11] Similarly, a mother I interviewed in Goma explained how the lack of material capacity to support her family has had an impact on her emotional relationship with her children:

> We love our children, of course we do. It's our culture to love them. We don't want them to go to the streets. But since we are unable to care for them, children decide to go themselves. I try to give my children moral guidance, to tell them not to steal, to listen to the

words of God. I give them a blanket to keep them warm, but they tell me they can't eat the blanket. Sometimes I go to bed as soon as I get home because I'm unable to face the questions and requests of my children. Sometimes I shout at them angrily in the hopes that they'll stop asking me for things.[12]

The lack of economic capacity to meet the material needs of their children has led to a perceived reduction of authority among parents, one of whom told me: "We are overwhelmed."[13] During interviews, fathers repeatedly expressed their frustration at no longer being able to effectively guide their children. Demoralized and disempowered, many parents explained that they are at a loss for how they might reassume their roles as primary protectors of their children. As another mother in Goma explained: "My husband is no longer here; it's so much harder for widows. I have five daughters, the four older ones all had babies at a young age. Already my youngest is becoming difficult—she's twelve years old."[14] It was clear in my discussions with parents that they wanted to do so much more for their children. One father explained what being a caring parent means to him: "It means giving our children what they need. Food first. Then schooling. Then counsel. As children, we were disciplined, and it was done with love and with an effort to keep us on the right path, to do the right thing. Even with all the difficulties in surviving today, this is what we keep trying to do."[15] Parents reported that despite their best efforts, they were increasingly unable to offer their children adequate support. According to many, their greatest concern was their difficulty paying their children's school fees. From 1990 to 1991, the state either no longer paid teachers' salaries, or paid a derisory amount, to those teachers who were on the state payroll. This began the now pervasive and entrenched practice of teachers' salaries being paid by parents.

Many of my conversations with parents evoked their sense of deep loss and desperation in not be able to fulfill their basic parenting obligations. Parents in Masisi Territory explained: "If we had the means, we would give everything for our children. We are just no longer able to."[16] Another group of parents linked their inability to support their children with unemployment and the lack of available basic social support services: "We have lost our capacity to care for our children. There are multiple illnesses in our families, we need first to pay for the hospital fees, for medication. These are recent problems—it didn't use to be like this. Before there were jobs, and we could manage, but not anymore."[17] The conditions of deepening poverty under which so many people live are preventing them from fulfilling their role as primary caregivers. This leaves their children to fend for themselves.

According to young people participating in this research, the inability of so many people to meet basic material needs has led to the collapse of the family structure: "The home is no longer a stable place. Fathers are no longer able to care for their families; they decide to abandon them."[18] The rising incidence of fathers abandoning their families was also articulated by adults and was usually explained by the lack of means to support the family: "The father goes away looking for work, and then just doesn't come back."[19]

Young people also explained how material constraints have led to increased family conflicts, usually expressed as competition over scarce property and landownership rights. In a discussion with a group of young men, they explained: "If a parent dies, other members of the family will do everything to try to chase you out, to get your parents' land from you. You'll be left with nothing."[20] The risks associated with the breakdown of the

family unit and competition over property were exemplified in
the narrative of a seventeen-year-old in Goma:

> My father left my mother; he abandoned me and my sister. Eventu-
> ally, my mother remarried and we lived for a while in her husband's
> house. When her second husband died, his family came to chase
> my sister and me away. They told us we had no right to live in
> the house left by their brother. Our mother said that we would have
> to leave her. She told us: "If you stay in this house, then I'll be
> chased away too. Your irresponsible father refuses to allow me to
> live with him. I have to protect the house and the things left by my
> husband...."
>
> So my sister and I found ourselves in the street. My sister was
> hired by a woman as a maid and she still lives with her today. As for
> me, I spend my nights in small shops abandoned by their owners.
> Each morning I go to construction sites around Goma to see if I
> can find work, to assist a mason or to transport water for the build-
> ers. When that doesn't work, I spend my days at the cement facto-
> ries to transport bags of cement to the market or to other customers.
> At the end of the day I might earn 500 Fc [Congolese francs] or
> 1000 Fc [US$0.5 or US$1]; this amount is never enough to eat well.[21]

As has been demonstrated in other war-affected contexts, social
support is weakened by the reduced availability of resources
and the inability of people to invest in and exchange with each
other.[22] This is equally true in the DRC, where deeply entrenched
poverty and structural violence make accessing social support
much more challenging for young people.

Economic difficulties are worsened by continuing military
insecurity, associated population displacement, the inability to
cultivate or harvest land, insecurity of trade routes, and the lack
of employment opportunities. Regular looting or extortion by
armed elements positioned throughout eastern DRC also means
that a family's food or material gains are dramatically reduced.

As explained by some parents: "At each barrier we have to pay at least 200 Fc [US$0.20], plus other taxes. If five bags of rice have been harvested, by the time we get to the market, there are only two bags left."[23]

Armed attacks on homes and villages also have a profound impact on people's survival capacities. The looting of personal property can easily break the tenuous economic hold maintained by families living on the edge of survival: "During the war, our goods were all pillaged, everything was taken. We were left with nothing."[24] Following a period of displacement to escape fighting in Masisi Territory, one seventeen-year-old girl explained, "When we returned home, we found our house destroyed."[25] The looting of animals in rural areas further weakened coping capacities: "We were left completely poor after the pillage, we were left at zero."[26]

CONTEMPORARY PATRONAGE

Struggling with unemployment, poverty, displacement, and instability, families are no longer able to offer the support they once did. Consequently, other strategies are being sought by young people, none more so than finding a patron. In a social system that has been transformed by monetized exchange, generalized conditions of poverty, and the distrust associated with decades of political and structural violence, the once strictly regulated patronage ties have become informalized and often violent, reducing options for self-protection and offering little support in ensuring long-term survival.

The work of James C. Scott, political scientist and author of *The Moral Economy of the Peasant,* lays the foundation for understanding the relationships that govern many aspects of rural life, including patrimonialism and patronage. Patronage is traditionally defined as a relationship of exchange, usually based on "dyadic (two-person) ties involving a largely instrumental friendship in which an individual of higher socioeconomic status (patron) uses his own influence and resources to provide protection or benefits, or both, for a person of lower status (client) who, for his part, reciprocates by offering general support and assistance, including personal services, to the patron."[27] As noted by Scott, in contexts of economic adversity and political uncertainty, the client's survival is constantly under threat, thus making patronage support an essential aspect of ensuring one's personal security. Patronage relations tend to dominate in contexts where there are significant wealth and power inequalities and where there are no institutionalized guarantees of physical security for those in the position of weakness.

In such a system, portraying weakness, subordination, and deference can increase one's chances of gaining protection and assistance from those with greater power: "Where subsistence needs are paramount and physical security uncertain, a modicum of protection and insurance can often be gained only by depending on a superior who undertakes personally to provide for his own clients.... When one's physical security and means of livelihood are problematic, and when recourse to law is unavailable or unreliable, the social value of a personal defender is maximized."[28]

Throughout modern Congolese history, patronage has been a dominant feature of daily life and public administration. In the precolonial era, traditional authority over the control of land was held by local chiefs, who presided over geographic areas that coincided with unified language and identity groups. People would pay regular tribute to their chief in exchange for access to land, while supporting a "local moral economy" in which loyalty was offered in exchange for protection.[29] Eventually these traditional patron-based systems of rule became formalized as the Native Authorities in which traditional chiefs were largely subsumed within the colonial machinery.[30]

As explained elsewhere in discussions of colonial governance throughout sub-Saharan Africa, the colonial administration used the existing patronage system to its advantage in order to extract the "maximum resources from the least financial and coercive expenditure."[31] While constructing themselves in the "paternal image," the Belgian authorities contributed to the long process of weakening "the powers of the local lineage chiefs over land attribution replacing those by more individual and monetarized transactions."[32] As described by historian Crawford Young in 1965, colonial administrators considered themselves the parents of their Congolese subjects, whom they thought of as "big children" in need of guidance through their stage of "arrested adolescence."[33] The power differential between colonial administrators and Congolese "subjects" was maintained through the use or threat of violence, placing the majority of the population in a position of relative weakness.

Ascending to power in 1965 in the newly named Zaire, Mobutu Sese Seko further entrenched the state use of patronage ties for asserting his control over the country. While consolidating his position as "father of the nation," Mobutu also skillfully positioned Zaire as a key Cold War client in a global political economy of patronage. Any well-functioning patronage system relies essentially on the flow of material goods, and Mobutu was able to ensure political loyalty within Zaire by balancing elite interests with the profits of Western munificence that he had amassed in exchange for his Cold War services. At the national level, Mobutu expertly "converted economic assets into a stock of political resources for (re-) distribution to those who had shown political loyalty."[34] These political elites in turn used their material gains to manage their own patron-based networks, a system that was replicated down to the most local levels.

A functioning patronage system is not based on one person but "involves a network of patron-client relationships transcending the entire society." Anthropologist Henrik Vigh further draws the link between the strength of patronage ties and ethnic politics: "Part of the resilience of patrimonialism is that, contrary to popular belief, it is not centred on one primary patron but involves a network of patron-client relationships transcending the entire society. As such, ethnicity and patrimonialism strengthen each other, as ethnicity provides ready-made structures for the distribution of resources and invests it with moral obligation."[35]

Examining how elite interests within patronage-based systems are balanced, social anthropologist Alex de Waal introduces the concept of a "political marketplace," where political loyalty comes at a price, where the successful patron is the one who is able to effectively respond to market prices for loyalty. In this form of "retail patronage politics," inclusivity is key to ensuring the sustainability of the system. De Waal explains how in Zaire "those out of favour [would] focus on how to return to favour under the existing system.... It was a cheaper way of maintaining the system and had the advantage that it could prevent those who were in favour from being able to build a durable patronage system of their own, and to that degree it was sustainable."[36] As highlighted by de Waal, Mobutu perfected the balancing act among elites, giving and taking favor in a sufficiently predictable manner to manage elite interests.

Until the late 1980s, Mobutu had been largely able to satisfy elite interests due to the largesse of Western governments, as well as with the revenues collected from the extraction of mineral resources. By the end of the Cold War, however, Western funding dried up, while decades of misuse and lack of investment in the mining infrastructure left by the Belgians meant that Mobutu's main sources of wealth began to disappear. No longer having the capacity to pay his patron debts, Mobutu started to lose control of the patron-client equilibrium he had so carefully maintained.[37]

Consequently, elite interests were able to more freely engage in their own forms of predation, as the army and actors in state institutions increasingly used the authority of their public positions to increase their private gain. As the Zairian patron-state began its "retreat from citizens," agents of the state—from soldiers to civil servants to teachers and other service providers transformed patronage in ways that were increasingly dysfunctional.[38]

The breakdown of Mobutu's patron state did not lead to the collapse of Congolese patronage system overall, however. Rather, patronage in Zaire was transformed, adapting both to the increased importance of monetized exchange and to higher levels of violence. In terms of monetization, the Congolese transformation reflected processes that similarly occurred elsewhere in sub-Saharan Africa, where the "over-monetarization of everyday life" began to take hold.[39]

In the early 1990s, the material goods and money formerly bestowed by patrons became even more restricted as a result of shifts in global market prices and the rising cost of food and other goods. According to Gérard Prunier, while per capita income had been measured at US$630 in 1980, by the early 1990s "per capita income had fallen so low that is was now hard to measure ... between US$78–US$88."[40] The resulting economic scarcity meant that cash became the essential tool for survival, thus shifting the functions of social support previously fulfilled by patronage relations.

The shifting nature of Congolese patronage relationships had been documented in 1972 by René Lemarchand and Crawford Young in a written correspondence in which they discussed the challenges of understanding clientelist relations in post-independence Zaire "when all is fluidity, when the networks are far more ephemeral, when mutual costs and benefits of maintenance of particular patron-client sets are apparently recalculated very frequently, and on the basis of very short-run contingencies."[41]

As patronage support became less reliable, an "individualistic, acquisitive 'capitalist lifestyle'" came to dominate.[42] The legitimacy and primacy of material wealth became necessary not only for the expression of political power but also within social culture, as the popular prerogative shifted toward one of *devenez riche rapidement*. Moving away from the traditional norms of family- and kin-based social support, where trust has an important regulating role, the new social norm that came to dominate Congolese social relations was that "a man is more of a man when he has more wealth."[43]

Displays of wealth have become more important in contemporary Congolese life, even as the economic situation has worsened and material resources have become scarcer for the majority of the population. Such adverse conditions have led to a situation where social relations are increasingly commoditized, where individuals help each other with the expectation of something being received in return.[44] Demonstrating how an individualizing market economy and deepening economic adversity have come to dominate contemporary capacities for coping with adversity, Nzeza Bilakila explains how contemporary social support functions in Kinshasa: "Poverty is psychologically transformed into despair solidarity. While the Kinois [people from Kinshasa] are able and willing to extend psychological support, financial and material constraints limit this solidarity to a pragmatic system of exchange. People help each other primarily if they expect something in return. Debt, whether it be in the form of a loan, a service rendered or a favour, will ultimately have to be redeemed."[45] Poverty has clearly had a transformative effect on social support throughout the DRC, and social coping capacities have been further weakened by political violence.

Although violence—or at least the threat of violence—is implicit in the patronage equilibrium as it preserves relations of power, violence has become increasingly dominant in defining social relations in the DRC, and particularly in the Kivus, where extortion, repression, and predation have come to replace the social controls of reciprocity. Although threats were also implicit in patronage relationships of the Mobutu era, "the difference between the current situation and the historical patterns of patrimonialism is the systematic use of violence."[46] If traditional patron-based systems implied a relationship of trust, in the Kivus violence and coercion have broken down expectations of trust between patrons and clients, a strain that has been compounded by decades of conflict and general uncertainty about future survival options.

Despite these shifts, the patron figure remains a powerful social, political, and economic force in the contemporary DRC. Today, patrons are identified as those in positions of power, such as administrators or government authorities, or anyone who can control or gain access to material resources. The way in which individuals navigate these reconceived patterns of patronage was demonstrated clearly to me by Mr. Bisa. He was the only driver I could find in Bukavu who was willing to take me to and from my fieldwork site in Bunyakiri during a relatively tense period of military operations. During our trips, Mr. Bisa would usually exhaust me with his endless stream of demands for a job for him, for his brother, and for his wife, and also, if possible, for some money to pay his children's school fees as well as their unpaid medical bills. Usually I would listen to his barrage of requests for help with patience and attempts at diversion. But one day, the discussion offered me unexpected insights into the complexity of engagement in patronage relationships. As I subsequently recorded in my fieldwork diary:

> Mr. Bisa's driving was more erratic today than usual, and I wondered how many beers he'd drunk while I'd been with the kids. He began his job-money-help tirade as soon as we started our drive back and was even more insistent. Despite my best efforts at distraction and avoidance, he repeated his now firmly established truth that I had completely failed in my promise to find him a real job so that, at last, he could properly take care of his family. Eventually the conversation strayed, and for a while we settled into silence.
>
> As we neared the end of our trip and entered the early evening traffic in Bukavu, Mr. Bisa spotted a red Pajero in front of us. Dodging the deep holes of the Bukavu streets, the weaving motorbikes, and the suddenly crossing children, Mr. Bisa pushed heavily down on the accelerator and began to urgently and repetitively sound the car horn. Excitedly he turned to me: "That's my *député* [a Provincial Assembly representative]. There he is! He's the one we elected from our area!"
>
> In the most determined driving I'd yet experienced with him, Mr. Bisa managed to draw even with the Pajero at the next intersection. He reached over me, rolled down my window and—as I

shrank back in my seat as far as I possibly could—extended his body over mine and reached his arm out the passenger window toward the representative's car, now blocked from moving forward by our car.

"*Député! Député! Bonjour!*" I sat back to witness Mr. Bisa's outpouring of verbal prostrations. The representative's face could have masked any number of shifting feelings, but within a couple of seconds settled into a smile. The elaborate and extended verbal exchange which proceeded over me included several requests from Mr. Bisa for "a small thing," a "Fanta," and on it went. Eventually, the representative reached into his shirt pocket and pulled out 500 Fc [US$0.50], which he extended out from his window into Mr. Bisa's open hand. Our drive home could at last continue.

I was amazed. "Mr. Bisa ... really? Did you really just beg your representative for 500 Fc?" In my ensuing barrage of questions, I tried to be make sense of his overt display of weakness and desperation. I wanted to understand how he could beg so blatantly for such a small amount of money, especially as I was paying him more than US$100 for that day of work alone.

"No, no, Claudia, it's not like that at all. You must understand. He is our *député*. He expects me to beg from him. If I didn't it would be as if I was insulting him, as if I didn't consider him to be an important person."

That I understood: make the Big Man feel big. But Mr. Bisa continued with his explanation, offering an analysis which I had not considered before, and which reflected his skillful manipulation of available opportunities and his longer-term perspectives on survival: "Because I ask him for help, he understands that I depend on him. Today 500 Fc means nothing. We both know that. But one day in the future I may really need him. Because he has helped me today, he has accepted the role of being my patron. Tomorrow, if one of my children is ill, or we have another kind of emergency at home, I will go to him. Because he has already accepted his role as my father today, he will feel responsible for giving the money when I really need it in the future."

While I initially considered Mr. Bisa to be expressing the "dependency complex" long critiqued in sub-Saharan Africa, I eventually realized that through his deliberate positioning of vulnerability, he was investing in a much more nuanced dynamic of power and weakness.[47] No longer simply a story about Big Men exuding power over the poor, through Mr. Bisa's explanation I could now understand the self-projection of weakness and dependence as a sophisticated tactic within longer-term social coping processes.

In the system of patronage that dominates everyday life in the Kivus, the reliance on weakness and subordination by individuals, including young people, aims to increase access to material benefits and protection. Yet, as shown in the case of Mr. Bisa, the amount of material support that may be offered by the patron will usually be insignificant in the face of the limited opportunities and extreme demands imposed by the conditions of poverty and structural violence. Although Mr. Bisa was hopeful that his representative would be able to help him should he ever find himself in a position of desperate need in the future, it is not certain that such assistance would be forthcoming. In the DRC, the needs of most of the population are so great—and daily survival so precarious—that no patron, despite having the best of intentions, could meet the expectations placed on him by all of those seeking his help.

The inability of today's patrons to satisfy the growing material needs of those in positions of comparative weakness means that patronage ties have become a less dependable form of social support. Yet, contrary to what might be expected, the lack of dependability of patronage ties in the DRC does not render such ties obsolete. Rather, people have become even more desperate to gain access to the now scarcer material resources that are distributed among a smaller number of people.

My young research collaborators were aware of the inherent injustice and inequality of this system, yet the sense of dejection in their accounts was less about the system itself and more about the unlikelihood that they would ever be able to gain access to it. For them, entering into the highly unfavorable dyad of contemporary patron relationships represented the only possibility of eventually gaining access to resources, jobs, or other forms of protection that they require. In this way, buying into a social system of exclusion, inequality, and weakness represented their only chance for improving their short-term survival prospects. Many of their coping tactics were therefore directed to positioning themselves as a client to potential patrons, emphasizing their weakness with the hope that they might be able to access the needed resources that would aid in their daily coping efforts.

## TACTICAL WEAKNESS

Portrayals of weakness as part of efforts to gain access to patronage featured regularly during my time in the DRC as the young people I knew and worked with remained aware of my position of relative power and thus of my potential to eventually serve as their patron. This was especially noticeable among some of my research participants in the aid-saturated context of Bukavu, where many of our early casual discussions would include references to money and its scarcity. With time, I could move beyond overt expectations of patronage with most of my research participants as they came to realize that I did not have the means they expected all *mzungus* (white people) to have. As we developed relationships that became more substantive, eventually their mention of money and material needs subsided. However, a few of them—especially those who became more deeply involved as key research participants over the months—were clearly investing in a relationship with me for the longer term, a relationship they hoped might eventually lead to some greater benefit.

One of my research participants, Michel, remained persistent in his requests for my patronage. He tried multiple tactics, initially during our conversations and eventually in writing:

Dear Madame Claudia

At the age of 10, I lost one of my parents. I became an orphan of my father. From that age survival became very difficult. The death left the whole family in a situation of extreme hardship. My mother suffers an illness of her stomach and hypertension.

The five children in the family came under my charge when I was 10 years old, when I was still in the second year of primary school. At that age I began to pay my school fees and the school fees for my younger siblings. I would look for small jobs, transporting rocks or collecting sand to sell so that I could find the money to pay for all of us.

Today I am 23 years old and I'm trying by all means possible to find the money to be able to finish my secondary school diploma. But the responsibilities I am faced with are so great, and they are multiplying. I don't know how we will manage anymore.

I ask for your help in finding a small job. Any job that would allow me to continue studying. I pray that you will receive this with my civic and patriotic feelings and pledge that this information is sincere.

Michel

This letter contains all the elements that I had come to expect in the many letters I had received in my years living in sub-Saharan Africa. Although there were individual variations in such requests for my patronage, these written narratives usually recounted the death of a parent, an illness, helpless children needing care, school fees needing to be paid, an expression of willingness to work, and—the motivation for the writing of the letter itself—a desperate moment when survival itself was in question. They were crafted in a way that aimed to appeal to my own sense of morality, projecting an obligation that, over the years and unfortunately for Michel, I had become less susceptible to accepting.

During my review of the patronage literature, I was surprised to discover that this formulaic patron-request letter not only is a tool used by young people in conflict-affected sub-Saharan Africa but also has served as a tool throughout modern history in highly divergent contexts. In his historic analysis of thousands of letters written by individuals in Florence in the fifteenth century, sociologist Paul McLean demonstrates how the patron letter was a tool that was frequently deployed by individuals in positions of relative weakness who sought favors from those in positions of power. The letters analyzed by McLean send the "mixed signals ... typical of patronage interaction, mingling expressions of deference with claims to desert" while proclaiming in desperation that "I have no other recourse but to you."[48]

This unexpected similarity in tactics used to gain patron support illustrated to me how individuals use their positions within society to support their own coping mechanisms and how these mechanisms reinforce people's positions of weakness. In both the contemporary Kivus and Renaissance Florence, the tactics employed by individuals are determined by the structures in which they live. By tracing the patron-request letters over time, McLean shows how the requests contained in the letters adapted and shifted during phases of war making and tax collecting, becoming part of the complex processes of state formation. The letters exemplified "the widespread Florentine strategy of relying on personal relationships *both* as a defense against the demands of the state *and* as a means of remaining an active member of it. Florentine citizens were thus not merely subjects or 'victims' of the state, but also its custodians."[49]

Similarly, the way in which young people continue to engage with contemporary patronage systems in the Kivus—despite these systems' general lack of benefit—reflects how they become the custodians of an unequal and dysfunctional system. According to the young people I worked with, the possibility of a brighter future can only be envisioned after finding "someone who will take care of you."[50]

For young Congolese people, the patron features prominently in any success story. Any narratives about effective coping usually mentioned being helped by a patron to find a job or to pay school fees; it is impossible for young people to imagine another way out of their difficult life situation. The aspirations of a twenty-year-old man in Bukavu were echoed by many: "I dream of someone taking me out of this situation."[51] Young people often perceived that their daily conditions, for better or for worse, depended on others.

Effectively engaging in such dynamics of dependence requires astute capacities for appraisal and flexible responses, and the ability to be sensitive to imbalances in power. While in some cases young people are successful in gaining entry to a patron-client relationship and consequently can receive the desired material support to pay their school or medical fees or be given an opportunity to work, usually their efforts to find a patron are unsuccessful. Given the increasing needs of a population living in adverse conditions, there are just too many clients who need support to keep the patronage system functioning in a beneficial way for young people. Yet a lack of success in finding a patron does not stop young people from continuing to invest in this exploitative system. Buying into a social system of exclusion and inequality usually represents their only chance for improving their short-term survival prospects.

One manifestation of the ambiguity of effective, present-day coping is the widespread reliance on weakness and victimhood to access material support. This tactical coping strategy arguably contributes to further weakness and dependence. Such a tactical use of vulnerability has been termed "victimcy" by Mats Utas, explained as "a form of self-representation by which a certain form of tactic agency is effectively exercised under the trying, uncertain, and disempowering circumstances that confront actors in warscapes," usually to gain access to assistance and services.[52] Victimcy requires a refined capacity for evaluating differentials in power and the possibilities that may be presented through portrayals of weakness. It is a concept that describes the ways that individuals present themselves depending on their reading of the audience they face. Victimcy is a tactic that consciously interacts with the environment and is particularly relevant in contexts of high inequality.

Conscious of these power differentials, young people rely on victimcy to make the most of available opportunities provided by external actors. In the aid-saturated context of the Kivus, international humanitarian assistance is usually directed only toward those considered to be the "most vulnerable." Young people in the Kivus are aware of these categorizations and understand that portraying themselves as vulnerable is likely to increase their chances of receiving access to aid. Victimcy thus becomes a key tool in the coping repertoire of young people.

While the tactical adoption of weakness helps young people to gain access to aid on an opportunistic basis, the reliance on such tactics generally dictates a situation where "the weaker party conforms to the same rationality as the dominant party."[53] By conforming to the dominant rationality of vulnerability, young people reinforce their position of victimhood and dependence. Portraying oneself as weak and helpless may increase one's chances of receiving material assistance from external actors in the short term, but there is a real longer-term risk that one's own position of weakness and vulnerability is reinforced. Although young people are tactically choosing to portray themselves as weak to increase their opportunities in facing the challenges of everyday survival, by doing so they are also reinforcing patterns of dependence, weakness, and inequality. Consequently, their tactical engagement with these structures—the only survival option available to most—contributes to their continued entrenchment in conditions of poverty, and thus to their own inability to overcome the unending subjugation of violence.

# CHAPTER SIX

# Meanings of Violence

## MEANING ATTRIBUTION

Throughout my time in the DRC, I struggled to comprehend the violence that I witnessed and documented daily. I would feel rage and despair as people shared accounts of their experiences. My unspoken response to the abjection, defeat, and submission I persistently witnessed was not far from fury: Why wouldn't they get angry? How could they just continue to accept the unacceptable? Yet the very people who were surviving this violence each day would recount their experience with a sense of quiet and defeated acceptance.

To help me make sense of this, I found the psychological literature on meaning attribution most helpful. The term "meaning attribution" describes how people "think about their experiences and how they incorporate them into their overall schema of themselves, their environment, and their relationships with other people."[1] Attributing meaning offers us a sense coherence to our experiences, and thus psychologically protects us. According to the meaning-making psychological model:

> People are meaning-makers insofar as they seem compelled to establish mental representations of expected relations that tie together elements of their external world, elements of the self, and most importantly, bind the self to the external world. When elements of perceived reality are encountered that do not seem to be part of people's existing relational structures, or that resist relational integration, these inconsistent elements provoke a "feeling of the absurd," a disconcerting sense of fundamental incongruity that motivates people to re-establish a sense of normalcy and coherence in their lives.[2]

Such coherence is an essential element of how we might effectively cope with adversity and to make sense of our experiences. How people give meaning to extreme experiences of violence was studied extensively after World War II, including by Austrian neurologist Viktor Frankl, himself a Holocaust survivor. Frankl's foundational studies with other survivors of the concentration camps revealed that a "will to meaning" is the primordial drive that motivates human experience.[3]

More recently, psychologists working with young people in contexts of political violence have confirmed that long-term well-being is directly linked to the meaning that young people attach to their experiences. A sense of coherence and predictability between one's internal and external environment is essential and is derived from a range of sources, including social belonging, a sense of life purpose and responsibility to others, as well as political or religious ideology.[4]

One of the most powerful constructs of meaning in the Kivus is identity. As described by Patrick Chabal and Jean-Pascal

Daloz, identity is represented by "a set of beliefs, values and subjective perceptions which are both eminently malleable and susceptible to change over time."[5] Identity-based politics in the Kivus are always simmering and easily manipulated by political entrepreneurs. While used to stoke fear and incite violence, the resulting "us" versus "them" categorizations can also help people to derive meaning and coherence from experiences of suffering and loss. Identity-based meanings of violence are at once psychologically protective and part of the dynamic through which violence is reproduced and retransmitted.

Throughout the Congolese conflicts, Mayi-Mayi militia clearly manifested the linkages between identity and violence. Usually Mayi-Mayi are described as local heroes who protect their communities from aggressive perpetrators, and my young research participants often mentioned them in their accounts of violence. For many, these local militia represented the local force of resistance to outside aggression, and thus a source of pride and meaning.

Young people in a small town of rural South Kivu explained how the Mudundu 40 (M40) Mayi-Mayi group became mobilized during the 1998–2003 war in response to constant attacks and pillage by the RCD and the FDLR forces:

> With all the attacks, a movement called the M40 was created. They fought against the Hutu. They pushed the Hutu away from here. After a while, the RCD arrived. The M40 fought against them too but were beaten by the RCD. For six months we were all displaced in the forest. The RCD undertook exactions, pillaged the hospital and the church. In the forest, the M40 reorganized itself to fight against the RCD. They managed to chase the RCD away and the population was able to return. We lived with the M40, they protected us. From the south M40 fought the Hutu, and from the north it fought the RCD.[6]

Mayi-Mayi have been described as a bottom-up solution to social and economic marginalization within a political landscape where elite interests rarely correspond to local needs and where the Congolese state offers little protection to the population.[7] Yet, while mobilizing in self-defense, contemporary Mayi-Mayi movements are also critiqued for pursuing their own material interests, often enacting violence against the very population they claim to protect.

Over time, by regularly attacking civilian populations, Mayi-Mayi would lose their moral high ground. This is turn would tarnish the protective role otherwise attributed to them. Consequently, the meanings of violence as protective and thus psychologically helpful would begin to lose their hold. As one fourteen-year-old explained: "During the war, we had a little money because my father had been able to sell six of our cows. But then one day the M40 came and took our money. They burned our house. We fled.... The M40 used to force us to work for them. If we refused, we'd be imprisoned."[8] The sense of disillusionment over having lost control of the heroic narrative evoked sadness and a sense of defeat among my young research participants. No longer able to conceive of the Mayi-Mayi as "local protectors" against "foreign aggressors," they acknowledged that mobilization to violence was also about access to material resources. Such a pragmatic analysis left them feeling more troubled and less able to make sense of the experiences of violence they had survived than would a narrative that clearly identified them as victims being protected by the Mayi-Mayi.

One afternoon I was traveling in a heavily militarized rural area of Masisi Territory, a zone where most people survive through subsistence farming and daily wage labor. It is a fertile, resource-rich area where continuing cycles of violence have led to repeated waves of population displacement, and where heavy militarization has reinforced a climate of fear and distrust. Here I met a traditional chief of Hunde identity who explained how a history of local land conflict had become entrenched in poverty, inequality, and insecurity:

> Poverty here has become extreme. The land has been taken from its former owners. Traditional chiefs no longer have authority, we have been relegated to the sidelines. We, the Congomani—the Bahunde, Nande, and Nyanga—have been forced off our land. Outside the city, the countryside is controlled by the Hutu. The Hutu also want to control the Hunde.
>
> Before it was OK, we used to recognize the Tutsi and the Hutu as foreign visitors, we accepted them here. But then they thought they could have power over the autochthons. They had money, they had the cows.
>
> Our first war was in 1965 in this Hunde area. The second war was in 1992, again between the Hutu and the Hunde. After this war, the Hutu wanted to kill all the Hunde. The arrival of Hutu from Rwanda in 1994 helped them in their efforts. Then the Rwandan Tutsi came to chase after the *génocidaires*. The Tutsi were so strong. They believed that the Hunde supported the Hutu, so we were all targeted.
>
> Now things are not good for the Congomani. I am a chief and even I can't access my land anymore. I have one hundred hectares of land that I am unable to cultivate. What can I do? I've tried to go through the judicial system to get my land back. But when I go there, I am threatened. They hint I could be killed.[9]

By blaming Rwanda for the violence in eastern DRC and effectively focusing public attention and blame on the violent "other," Congolese political elites at the local, provincial, and national levels successfully deflect attention away from their own lack of effective leadership and inability to fulfill their obligations to the population they are responsible for governing.

Serving as a useful tool to distract potential opposition away from the dysfunctions of the state toward an external "enemy," this blame enables those benefiting from the violence to continue to do so unchecked.

At the individual level, blame can be used to explain a situation in which one feels powerless, providing a sense of coherence for understanding systemic injustice. Yet what happens when blame is not ascribed? As I would learn, the refusal to blame an "other" can lead to a perilous existential place where rage risks taking over. One afternoon in 2011, I was in a village not far from that of the Hunde chief, conducting a project evaluation on behalf of an international NGO. Included in my evaluation methodology were group interviews, which I convened in a small *pointe d'écoute*, or "listening point." This was a clubhouse of sorts, a small room that had been constructed with planks, where children were encouraged to visit in case they needed help or psychosocial support from a trained community support worker.

In the middle of a discussion with a group of women from the village, a man suddenly burst in, shouting: "Madame, I must talk to you!" His arms were raised, and his eyes were bright. Within a few seconds, my colleagues and a few young men who had been lingering outside came in to restrain him. They tried to hold the man's arms and force him out of the small room, but he became even more agitated and shouted, pleading to be able to speak with me. Risking the possibility of being punched in the face, I approached him and reached out my hand. I asked him if he would like to sit down.

Almost instantly, he was calm. I convinced the young men restraining him to release their hold. They replied in a protective attempt at dissuasion: "But he is crazy, Claudia. A totally

crazy man. A drunkard. You don't have to talk to him." I
insisted that I would like to hear him—we were in a place built
for listening, after all. I wanted to hear what he had to say.
They relented and grudgingly left us in the room. For the next
twenty minutes, this man, who introduced himself as a teacher,
recounted a story of hopelessness and anger in perfectly articulated French. Formerly a history teacher, he explained the desperate conditions in which he, his family, and the whole country
were living: "We have no human rights, Madame. Look at this!
Look at how we live! They say we are a democracy now in
Congo, but it is a dictatorship. Any time we try to stand up, we
get shot down. Look here, like you saw just now, any time I try
to speak, I am shut up. I am told that I have lost my mind. But
I have not. I know what I'm saying. Look at these conditions
of misery! Such misery. Suffering! Total suffering. We have no
rights. There is no justice." This man's narrative moved from
one human rights violation and indignity to another, from one
battle in Masisi to the next, and to the impacts of this violence
on the population. He described the breakdown of the schooling
system, his consequent unemployment, and the destitution into
which he had fallen.

Eventually the NGO driver came back in to tell me it was
time for us to leave because night would soon be falling and we
needed to return to town before curfew. The teacher became
agitated again and started raising his voice. I tried to assure him
that I had heard him, that I absolutely agreed with him that the
conditions in which the Congolese population was living were
outrageous and unacceptable. I told him that I would write the
story he had just recounted, that his words would find their way
to a bigger audience, and that at least his story would be read by
others.

I wanted to believe that my affirmations might have soothed his distress, but once I got into the NGO's Land Cruiser, he tried to block me from leaving. As we drove away, he stumbled after us on the dirt road, dust rising, still shouting after me with his arms in the air. Breaking the silence in the car as we drove back to the town, my colleagues wanted to assure me: "Claudia, don't worry about him. He's just a crazy old man." We returned to our silence as twilight quickly fell.

I did not know if my colleagues' response to the man we had met was based on embarrassment, a desire not to portray weakness to an outsider, or something else, but in effect, their assertion of his mental illness confirmed how one who does not cling to strategies of blame can easily, if gradually, be cast to the margins of society. The man's testimony made perfect sense to me, was completely logical, but he was labeled as "crazy" because his rage did not cohere with the dominant identity-based discourse. Consequently, his voice was silenced and remained unheard. By discerning and speaking out against the basic problems of political malgovernance and entrenched injustice, he had become marginalized. His unwillingness to accept the unacceptable human conditions recalled for me Hannah Arendt's assertion that "impotence breeds violence" and that only "where there is reason to suspect that conditions could be changed and are not, does rage arise."[10]

### DEFEATED BY VIOLENCE

Rather than expressing fury, most young people I knew expressed a deep sense of hopelessness about their perspectives for the future: "How do we look at the future? Life will always be like this. Or worse."[11] Frequently, young people would include in their narratives the phrase "that's just how it is." This acceptance was a willful act of submission resulting from a cognitive appraisal of the conditions they had learned they were powerless to change.[12] By imposing profound limitations on the possibilities for human self-realization, structural violence was closing in on young people's horizons. They knew their lives were proscribed by violence, yet they unable to do anything about it.

The concept of leveled aspirations emerged from studies relating to social reproduction theory and urban poverty in North America, tending to occur predominantly in situations where "poverty circumscribes the horizons of young people in such a way that reproduces social inequalities through a 'levelling' or 'depressing' of their aspirations."[13] This concept explains how individuals who live in socioeconomically adverse conditions, usually at the margins of an overall wealthier society, eventually "come to accept their own position and the inequalities of the social order as legitimate."[14] Poverty becomes entrenched and transmitted from one generation to the next as young people learn to aspire in ways that reinforce their disadvantaged position.

Young people growing up in conditions of poverty and inequality learn to yield to a future that offers few possibilities of positive change. As the poorest members of society come to accept their adverse life conditions, dignity risks being suppressed. Ethnographic research in urban settings in the United States shows how racial segregation, economic marginalization, and social alienation have transformed young people's aspirations; as Philippe Bourgois's ethnography of street culture among young Latino men in East Harlem shows, young people adapt to structural violence in ways that entrench their own positions at the socioeconomic margins of society.[15]

Young people in the DRC devote tremendous energy to overcoming the formidable challenges of surviving structural violence and the conditions that make their daily lives so difficult. Yet as they have spent their whole lives in this situation, they have come to accept as normal the adversity and the struggle. Such acceptance is evident in the narratives of young people who in general were not consoled by the possibility of a better future. One young woman explained: "All we know is suffering, there is still violence, still war and hunger. People are being killed. Roads are not built. There is no support for school fees. Nothing has changed for us. We are not free. There is little reason to believe that we ever will be."[16] Another girl described: "My life is difficult. Both of my parents are poor, we haven't been able to study. I'm the eldest of seven children—I'm seventeen years old now.... I try to find whatever work wherever I can. I work for whoever offers a job, carrying loads, cultivating in their fields.... Even though the war has ended here, life isn't easier. I see how hard my mother works. For me it's the same. It will always be the same, nothing changes."[17]

The interface between political and structural violence emerged clearly in the narrative of another research participant, Roger, who was twenty-one years old when I met him. His village had been attacked seven years earlier, an attack that led to the killing of many villagers, including his parents and sister. Roger and his older brother had fled to the town center, where they still lived due to the continued insecurity in the area. In our discussions, Roger often expressed his feelings of helplessness and frustration with having to depend on his older brother, who paid his school fees and provided him with a place to live. He wanted to start his own family, but was blocked by his lack of financial means:

I eventually want to have children, to have the means to feed them and educate them. But now my only priority is my schooling. If I have any luck, it would be to get a job. I'll probably be a teacher when I finish secondary school, though I really dream of going to university. As a teacher, maybe the government will pay me 30,000 Fc [Congolese francs, approximately US$30] a month, plus I'll get the 25,000 Fc from the school fees that the students have to pay. But then 10 percent of what I might earn I'd have to give back to the church that runs the school, plus more for the school's functioning. This would never be enough money to live on, not at all.[18]

The concept of leveled aspirations helps to illuminate the processes by which poverty becomes entrenched and transmitted from one generation to the next. Locked into repeating cycles, young people learn to aspire in ways that reinforce their disadvantaged position. Poverty is reproduced and transmitted to the next generation. Young people's lack of hope in a better future is translated into the choices they make and the risks they take, both of which are based on present-oriented calculations. Young people are so busy dealing with the challenges of each day that they cannot invest in any kind of improved future.

The structures of violence are systemically reinforced by the apparatus of the state, even—and perhaps especially—in the situation of extreme state weakness of the DRC. The way that state agents use their administrative power at the expense of those in a position of relative weakness was demonstrated by Vainqueur, whose name translates from the French as "victor," or "he who defeats." Vainqueur had been displaced from his home village as a child with his family and had lived along the roadside for most of his life. Overcrowded conditions at home and increasing tensions with his father's second wife had led Vainqueur and his brother to move into a two-room mud-brick house a few months before I first met him in 2010. To earn money to buy food and to pay his rent, Vainqueur's daily subsistence means were primarily restricted to daily wage labor such as carrying rocks and sand from the hills to the roadside or transporting materials between towns on market days.

Vainqueur is skilled in art—a rare talent in the Kivus, where access to quality formal education is exceptional. Vainqueur would often supplement his responses to my research questions and complement group discussions by drawing sketches or illustrations. He had trained himself in drawing and painting and had gained renown as the local artist, painting signs for local businesses or NGO projects whenever such opportunities presented themselves. To make the most of his talents, Vainqueur had recently tried to set up his own art shop. After having worked arduously at various daily wage labor jobs over many months, he had managed to save up just enough money to build a stall where he would be able to receive clients and perhaps generate small contracts. With painstaking preparation and great anticipation, he finally opened his shop.

Within the very first hours of opening his business, however, Vainqueur described how "the authorities came to me and demanded that I pay them." The authorities included the Direction Générale des Recettes Administratives, Judiciaires, Domaniales et de Participation, or the tax authorities; the Agence Nationale de Renseignements, or the state intelligence service; and the police. Exercising their separate powers, these state authorities demanded immediate payment of various taxes and fees. Vainqueur had no money to offer and knew that the authorities would be capable of imprisoning him until he or someone in his family would pay the requisite amount to ensure his release. Vainqueur was able to negotiate himself out of arrest but was left with no other choice than to close his shop.

Vainqueur's description of the event during our discussion was controlled and careful, yet the anger and helplessness he felt on recalling this experience were palpable in his expression and body language. Powerless to resist the structures of violence, Vainqueur had no choice but to submit to them. The aspirations that Vainqueur once nurtured for creating a better future for himself had been leveled by the forces of the violence in which he lived. Demonstrating Arthur Kleinman's "cascade of violence"— in which violence flows from the highest to the lowest levels of the political and social hierarchy—Vainqueur had to yield to the violence to ensure his own survival.[19]

Vainqueur reflected on the frustration he felt at his inability to advance, and would express his emotional and psychological sense of defeat. While he had once believed that his artistic talents would have opened up possibilities for a different kind of life, he had since lost this aspiration as he submitted to the forces of violence everywhere around him. His low morale permeated many of our conversations, and he still felt a sense of failure for not having been successful in realizing his dreams: "Now I'm twenty years old, I'm an adult.... Today I should be somewhere else in my life."[20] Despite his tremendous talent, he had learned that the structures of violence proscribing his present and his future were too powerful for him to take on. He told me: "I don't have any means to change things."

As demonstrated through Vainqueur's narrative and through the description of the failed student uprising in 2007, submission to violence does not just happen. Capacities for rational appraisal were evident; one local proverb my young research participants taught me was that "when the tree is too big to cut down, we learn to live with it."[21] In this way, submission has become the best way to cope with the structures of violence which they have learned they are unable to change. The long-term consequences of relying on submission have an evident effect on young people's capacities to envision a brighter future. Their lack of hope is translated into the choices they make and the risks they take, both of which are based on present-oriented calculations. Preoccupied with surviving in the present, young people are not able to engage with the structures of violence in ways that would challenge or change them in the long term. The dilemma presented is thus evident: the capacity to effectively cope with the structures of violence today becomes part of the dynamic that ensures the conservation of these structures in the future.

## HOPE AND FUTURE

The belief that the future might be better that the present offers people the courage to confront present difficulties. For many of the young people I knew in the DRC, hopelessness had closed in on their horizons, leaving them focused only on the toil of daily survival. One seventeen-year-old girl shared this narrative during our first biographical interview:

> I'm from Walungu Territory, a place where many people were massacred during the war. My father had gone to the mining areas of Burega [Shabunda Territory in South Kivu Province] many years ago. We stayed at home with our mother. She sold clothes in the market and would use the money from selling to buy our food. We didn't cultivate.
>
> One night the AFDL came to our house. They demanded money from my mother. The soldiers began to beat her, demanding that she give them money. She refused. We started crying. The soldiers took a cord to my mother's neck to strangle her, so I ran inside to find our money. I gave the money to the soldiers to try to free my mother. But they took my mother behind the house and tied her

up. They had machetes; they began to cut my mother's hands. We screamed and cried out for help. The soldiers threatened us, then threw gasoline on the walls of the house and set fire to it. They took us into the forest with them. They took our goat. They didn't rape me, but we had to stay with them.

In the morning we were able to run away. We returned to our village to find everything burned, even the remains of my mother, even her skin had disappeared. We found part of her left leg, her head. I told myself and my brothers and baby sister: "We cannot cry because this is what the world is like today."

Our [paternal] aunt learned of the attack. She came to get us and brought us to Bukavu to live with her. In 2004 there was the attack of Bukavu—it lasted one week. During the attack, many people fled. My aunt was caught in the fighting and was shot in the leg. I didn't understand how this could happen. I had lost my mother, my father had disappeared, now my aunt was seriously hurt. We didn't know if she would live.... After two months my aunt got out of the hospital, but with her injury, she was no longer able to work. She told us we would have to start working to support ourselves.

My two brothers were very young then, they were eight and ten years old—they went to the street. My little sister was still a baby, she hadn't even finished her vaccines. I didn't know what to do. My neighbor told me I should look for work washing clothes. I managed to find a woman whose clothes I could wash. She had so many clothes! I worked so hard, for so long, my arms ached, it was so painful! At the end of the day she gave me 500 Fc (US$0.50). I was so tired. I went back to my aunt, gave her the money, and she told me: "Continue, this is how life is."

One day I learned from an old friend from my village that my father had been killed by the AFDL during the war. He'd been buried on the side of the road, just like that. How I cried. I lost all hope then. I thought maybe I should die, I could drown myself, take a rope around my neck. But I knew that I shouldn't cry—I had my little sister to care for, she had only me.

Despite her great courage, this young woman did not believe that life would ever improve for her. However, she kept going because she was responsible for caring for her little sister. Bringing up a child—a sibling or one's own child or, in many cases, both—proved to be one of the most important motivating factors among the young people I knew, one of the few ways through which hope might be regained.

Thérèse was twenty-two years old when I first met her in April 2010. She was in her last year of secondary school and the mother of a six-year-old boy. She had been born and raised in the commercial center of Walungu, and her parents, who had been relatively wealthy traders before the war, continued to live there. Thérèse described her early childhood years with fondness; it had been a time when she and her sisters benefited from not only the material care of their parents but also their emotional support. Thérèse and her three sisters had all been sent to school, an exceptional situation in contemporary DRC, where many families are unable to pay their children's school fees.

According to Thérèse, her idyllic childhood ended with the 1998–2003 phase of the war, when Walungu became a central theater of combat between the FDLR and the RCD. It was during these years of FDLR and RCD fighting that Thérèse was abducted by elements of the FDLR. She explained her experience during her biographical interview: "Some things one can forget, and once forgotten, they are gone forever. But other things cannot be forgotten. I was in my fourth year of secondary school. It was 2003, I was 15½. On 1 August 2003, I was taken by the Interahamwe. I had to stay in the forest with them for seven months. I was able to escape on 7 March 2004, and I found my way home. I was already seven months pregnant by then."

Her narration of her abduction experience was brief, and in our many subsequent discussions, Thérèse would not again explicitly mention her time with the FDLR or her experience of captivity. In contrast, she frequently talked about the difficulties she faced with her family after her escape. On her return home, she was met by unexpected resistance. As she recalled: "My family told me repeatedly that I had to get rid of the pregnancy. They considered my unborn baby to be the enemy, *le serpent*. But I wanted to keep it. I believed it was God's will. I was hated by the whole family then; only my mother provided me with any emotional support. My family was so angry with me, they told me they lost their cows because I'd been raped. Cows are so important to [our people]." Despite the enormous pressure applied on Thérèse by her family, she refused to terminate her pregnancy. For her, keeping the baby was a way to assert some control over a situation that she had been powerless to prevent. In this way she was able to exercise the limited choice available to her to make the best of her situation despite the overwhelming force of violence she had survived.

The agency expressed by Thérèse was also linked to her spiritual faith. Thérèse considered her abduction, repeated rapes, and eventual pregnancy to be part of "God's will," a belief that helped her to accept and make sense of her experience. Her commitment to her unborn child also allowed her to cope emotionally with the violence she had survived, expressing itself as something like forgiveness for her perpetrators.

Within a few weeks of her baby's birth, Thérèse's family received a message from the FDLR that they were going to come back to take her son because they believed he belonged to the FDLR. To save herself and her child, Thérèse escaped to Bukavu, hoping that the anonymity of the city would offer them some protection. She moved in with an older sister and focused all her efforts on finding ways to support herself and her baby. The handouts from friends and family and the small amounts of money she might earn from working in a tailoring workshop contributed to her sister's family income, paying for their food, and also paid her son's primary school fees. With any amount of money that might be left over each month, Thérèse paid her own school fees; her aim was to graduate from secondary school and continue on to university. Thérèse would seize any opportunity, finding ways of surviving and making the most of the possibilities available to her.

Despite her remarkable capacities for coping, Thérèse was aware that she might not always be able to fend for herself and her son. Given the social structures that continue to subordinate women in the DRC, Thérèse believed that the stability and social acceptance she and her son needed to adequately survive could only be achieved if she could find herself a suitable husband. However, having been raped by an FDLR element and having had a son from that rape meant that Thérèse was subject to strong social stigma. To deal with this, she explained to her son and to any prospective suitors that he was her younger brother, and that she was responsible for raising him. By adopting this new narrative, Thérèse hoped that she might one day get married and begin a new life.

In the following years, Thérèse's capacities to meet her survival needs wavered, as the strains of the everyday became too much to sustain her dreams. By the end of 2011, Thérèse had dropped out of her second year of university because she was no longer able to afford the fees. The sister she and her son had been living with was struggling to support her own children and consequently had asked Thérèse to leave. Living with a friend, Thérèse was dedicating her time to earning enough money to support herself and her son. Her goal of completing her university education seemed to be falling out of reach, as more pragmatic choices had to be made.

By 2012, Thérèse was compelled to leave Bukavu because she could no longer afford the cost of living there. She returned to her hometown, where, despite the terrible family rejection she had experienced there years earlier, she could at least find work as a schoolteacher, a job she could do with her high school qualification. She moved in with a relative, and each week would send money to her older sister in Bukavu, who had finally agreed to care for Thérèse's son so that he could continue his primary schooling there. Thérèse considered her life chances to be regressing dramatically; from having dreamed of being a university graduate, she was returning to her village as a teacher. Despite her remarkable tenacity and intelligence, the prospects of a better life in the city were simply untenable.

By the end of 2013, Thérèse's prospects were again looking up. She told me with happiness that she had met a good man who had married her, and she had just given birth to a little girl. With a stable teaching job in her hometown and her son still studying in Bukavu, she could again begin to imagine a brighter future. Although her own aspirations had been adjusted downward, she had successfully emerged from an excruciatingly difficult period of her young life. Through her children, she had found renewed strength; with courage and faith, she believed that the future would be kinder to them.

### LIBERATION FROM VIOLENCE?

In late 2017, I received a weekly update from one of my research associates based in South Kivu. He is a committed human rights activist who tirelessly documents the violence and abuses that are part of everyday life in his territory. In that one weekly report alone he documented the following: a checkpoint with impoverished farmers taxed on the way to the market; two girls raped on their way home (the perpetrators were either government soldiers dressed up as rebels or else actually rebels; an investigation is ongoing); and a man killed by gunshot in his field by a police officer for unknown reasons (the policeman ran away and has not been heard from since). The report went on to detail recent attacks by the Raia Mutombuki Mayi-Mayi group on a nearby village involving looting, pillage, and torture. It also contained details of a nascent coalition of local Mayi-Mayi groups organizing to contest the government should presidential elections not go ahead as constitutionally mandated.

This was one week in one limited area of one territory in South Kivu. Variations on a theme, the same story line is repeated week after week, territory upon territory. This is life today for many Congolese. For some Congolese, last week was even worse; for others, next week will be. Young people have few plausible reasons to believe that life tomorrow will get any easier than today. The ways that violence is survived and passed down through generations have transformed young people and their perspectives for the future. Defeated, they have stopped trying to fight against a system they have learned will ultimately subject them.

Such submission has deep historical roots. As was once explained to me by a local authority in North Kivu: "This complacency, this unwillingness to change things, this acceptance of violence, it dates back to the history of colonialism. Then, we were taught to accept anything we were given. That's how we remain today."[22] In 1960, Prime Minister Patrice Lumumba took the stage at the Independence Day ceremony, just as King Baudouin of

Belgium handed control of the state apparatus to the newly formed Congolese government. Lumumba would be assassinated just two and a half months later, due to his perceived potential to transform violence.[23] His Independence Day speech was powerful testimony to the strength of a people who had suffered far too long:

> No Congolese worthy of the name will ever be able to forget that it was by fighting that [independence] has been won, a day-to-day fight, an ardent and idealistic fight, a fight in which we were spared neither privation nor suffering, and for which we gave our strength and our blood. We are proud of this struggle, of tears, of fire, and of blood, to the depths of our being, for it was a noble and just struggle, and indispensable to put an end to the humiliating slavery which was imposed upon us by force....
>
> We have known harassing work, exacted in exchange for salaries which did not permit us to eat enough to drive away hunger, or to clothe ourselves, or to house ourselves decently, or to raise our children as creatures dear to us....
>
> We have seen our lands seized in the name of allegedly legal laws which in fact recognized only that might is right....
>
> We have witnessed atrocious sufferings of those condemned for their political opinions or religious beliefs; exiled in their own country, their fate truly worse than death itself....
>
> Who will ever forget the massacres where so many of our brothers perished, the cells into which those who refused to submit to a regime of oppression and exploitation were thrown?
>
> All that, my brothers, we have endured. But we ... who have suffered in our body and in our heart from colonial oppression, we tell you very loud, all that is henceforth ended.
>
> The Republic of the Congo has been proclaimed, and our country is now in the hands of its own children.[24]

Despite Lumumba's vision for a country freed of violence's oppression, life conditions remain exceedingly dire for so many Congolese. I once asked one of my colleagues how she continued to endure such highly compromised, adverse conditions, not only as a child rights activist but also as a mother. She responded simply, in a voice that contained little defiance but that was full of strength and endurance: "We are Congolese."[25]

Any meaningful transformation of violence in the DRC will require the informed demand and concerted will for change at multiple levels. As was once written by Franz Fanon, structural and political change must be willed at the local, individual level: "The proof of success lies in a whole social structure being changed from the bottom up. The extraordinary importance of this change is that it is willed, called for, demanded. The need for this change exists in its crude state, impetuous and compelling, in the consciousness and in the lives of [men and women]."[26]

In recent years, a youth movement called Lutte pour le Changement (LUCHA) has been working to mobilize young people across the DRC to protest the delayed presidential elections.[27] Many of these young militants have been arrested for "inciting civil disobedience."[28] This youth movement and other forms of nonviolent resistance face systematic repression, their will to make change peacefully facing asphyxiation. The groundswell of resistance evoked by Fanon that would be required to truly transform violence in the DRC—the precursor to Congolese liberation—awaits somewhere still in the future.

# CHAPTER SEVEN

# The Myth of International Protection

## HUMANITARIAN ILLUSIONS

The terrible irony of adversity and extreme suffering in the DRC is that, for more than a century, the country has been the focus of concerted humanitarian attention and impassioned international drives to improve human conditions there. Despite these long-term efforts, the DRC remains one of the least developed countries on earth, its population among the world's poorest. In 2014, the UK Department for International Development provided an overview of contemporary socioeconomic conditions:

> Decades of conflict and corruption have left DRC chronically unstable, lacking infrastructure and social services, and falling far short of its economic potential. Notwithstanding steady economic growth over the past decade, per capita GDP remains at just 43% of what it was in 1980 and around 60% of the population live on less than $1.25 per day.... Seven out of 10 people in rural areas do not have access to safe drinking water. Almost 1 in 3 children under 5 are severely malnourished and only 63% of girls and boys aged 6–11 regularly attend primary school. The state is unable to either

provide security, or ensure protection for the whole population: violent conflict and instability continues in the east, where the largest UN mission in the world is attempting to provide some measure of civilian protection. Instability in DRC has already led to Africa's first major inter-state war and continues to pose a threat to the region. The consequence of this wide-scale instability is that the country continues to face one of the most complex and chronic humanitarian crises in the world.[1]

By the end of 2017, the most senior UN official overseeing international humanitarian responses at a global level described the "dramatic deterioration" of the situation in the DRC. He noted that in 2017, 1.7 million people had been forcibly displaced by violence, bringing the total number of internally displaced people in the DRC to 4.1 million, making it "the largest displacement crisis in Africa." He warned that 7.7 million Congolese were "severely food insecure" and that the DRC was sliding deeper into crisis: "As we enter into 2018, more than 13 million people require humanitarian assistance and protection—that's near 6 million more people than at the beginning of 2017. We suspect the number may further increase during 2018."[2] A press release issued by UNICEF in December 2017 detailed the humanitarian crisis in the Kasai region, where recent fighting had led to the death of thousands, the displacement of more than a million people, and widespread destruction.[3] At least four hundred thousand children under five were said to be suffering from severe acute malnutrition, on the verge of dying. Yet, despite these egregious conditions, "the situation in DRC is at risk of being ignored while it develops into the biggest emergency of 2018." *Hunger Road*, a short documentary by the BBC's Fergal Keane, showed harrowing images of extreme human suffering currently under way in Kasai province, with children dying in the arms of their helpless parents.[4]

As my doctoral supervisor, Zoë Marriage, had encouraged me more than a decade ago, in the face of such devastating suffering, it is necessary to go beyond outrage to interrogate the factors that contribute to making these untenable conditions so persistent. Why does this keep happening? This simple question is rarely asked and almost never answered in the humanitarian discourse. Yet questioning the causes of the DRC's continuing humanitarian crisis—despite the presence of a massive international humanitarian response—is an ethical imperative.

Deeper reflection on the "do no harm" principle among international actors is usually precluded by the humanitarian imperative to save lives—there is simply no space and not enough time to allow for such critical reflection. The frenetic, endless cycle of acting, then reacting, continues unabated in a country the UN has described as having "been in a state of acute emergency for two decades."[5] Such labels elide the evident fallacy: twenty years is no longer an "emergency." When I would pose questions to my humanitarian and protection colleagues about the inefficacy of our work, their first response would usually be to cast blame on the Congolese government's corruption and inability to respond to even the most basic needs of its population. They would assert: "It would be so much worse here without us." But what if the Congolese government's corruption and inability to respond to even the basic needs of the population are being perpetuated precisely because of the humanitarian presence?

The DRC has received billions of US dollars in humanitarian aid over the last two decades—one study calculated an average of US\$1.5 billion received in aid annually.[6] Even as the foundations of the chronic humanitarian crisis remain unaddressed, the dominant humanitarian logic is that more money will make for more effective responses. In his captivating history of modern processes of development—*The Great Escape: Health, Wealth and the Origins of Inequality*—Nobel Prize–winning economist Angus Deaton calls this the "aid illusion": the belief that more money will improve the situation.[7] The strong hold of this illusion is evident in the annual funding appeals led by the UN: the 2017 Global Humanitarian Appeal for the DRC was launched by the UN in December 2016 and warned that if US$812 million was not raised, the humanitarian situation would worsen.[8] By December 2017, only US$400 million of these funds had been pledged, and the situation was, in places, worsening. Assertions of the causal link between unresolved crisis and the funding gap thus seemed to hold.

Yet the problem is far deeper than the one depicted by such UN-led appeals. Examining the dilemma of international assistance and its impact on a state's capacity to uphold its duty to its citizens, Deaton carefully and systematically reviews the long-run implications of aid: "Large inflows of foreign aid change local politics for the worse and undercut the institutions needed to foster long-run growth. Aid also undermines democracy and civic participation, a direct loss over and above the losses that come from undermining economic development."[9] As Deaton compellingly argues, one of the main reasons that aid damages governments is that it precludes the state-citizen contract. Governments remain accountable to no one, while aid actors come in to fill the gaps. In this way, international interventions facilitate, if not encourage, governments to remain unaccountable to their populations.

The historic weakness of Congolese government institutions has meant that international humanitarian actors have systematically come in to provide the most basic of state services—the colonial-era missionary hospitals and schools have been replaced by international NGO health and education projects. These projects provide basic social services where the state does not. The weak state is thus enabled. As in other contexts labeled as "failed states," the DRC remains reliant on external aid, "condemned to perpetual crisis."[10]

The seemingly unending crisis should raise the alarm about the lack of accountability of international aid actors in the DRC. In recent years the UN humanitarian system has increased its focus on accountability, and efforts have been made to improve standards of internal efficiency and professionalism. For example, the Inter-Agency Standing Committee—the international coordinating mechanism for humanitarian interventions—has elaborated a cluster system that has helped to improve information sharing, coordinated operations, and more efficient humanitarian responses. The "Core Humanitarian Standard on Humanitarian Accountability," published in 2014, includes nine commitments and aims to "facilitate greater accountability to communities and people affected by crisis, and improve the quality of services provided to them."[11] Yet accountability remains upward-gazing, focusing on international donors instead of on the people the funds are intended to help.

To improve project efficiency and effectiveness, independent evaluators are sent in on big budgets to examine the effectiveness of project pertinence, coverage, sustainability, coherence, and impact. The framework of questions demands to know if the interventions responded to the needs and expectations of the "beneficiary" populations. Were the most vulnerable reached in equitable ways? Were the project outputs and outcomes coherent with the change that had been intended? Did the projects accord with government strategies and with human rights norms? Are impacts sustainable?

These questions, among hundreds of standardized others, are not bad. They are in line with global-level initiatives such as the 2016 World Humanitarian Summit, which aimed toward more effective delivery of aid, and the 2030 Agenda of the Sustainable Development Goals, which pushes for the eradication of poverty, inequality, and violence, ensuring that "no-one is left behind." Yet while such advances may contribute to conceptual clarity and resonate with the will to do good, the cognitive dissonance between what policies and standards uphold, and their impact on the ground, resonates painfully.

## PROTECTION, DENIAL?

This critique begs the question: So what is to be done? An analysis of what needs doing can only begin after one acknowledges that what is currently being done by international aid actors is simply not what is claimed. Mark Duffield offers a lucid, general critique of development aid: "The benevolence with which development cloaks itself—its constant invocation of rights, freedom and the people—conceals a stubborn will to manage and contain disorder rather than resolve it."[12]

The dissonance between protection discourse and lived experiences is as evident in the DRC today as it was when I first began my protection work there in 2006. A question posed by one young person remains relevant: "Why do the UN and NGOs only respond to victims, but not try to stop the violence itself?"[13] While protection actors scramble to denounce the newest wave of violence, well-intentioned interventions serve to distract from the deeply political factors from which they have emerged. The very political origins of the violence are thus not seen, or are ignored, then reinforced, and on it goes with little change in the lives of the people whom protection actors aim to assist. Arundhati Roy discussed this in the context of NGO work in India, where such superficial interventions act "like the whistle on a pressure cooker. They divert and sublimate political rage and make sure that it does not build to a head."[14]

In the last decade, there has been an increased focus on the protection of civilians in conflict-affected contexts, as enshrined in the global "Responsibility to Protect" framework. This framework grew out of the protection crises of the 1990s, notably the Rwandan genocide and the Srebrenica massacre, each perpetrated despite the presence of UN peacekeepers.[15] In recent years, the term "protection" has come to the forefront of humanitarian discourse. According to the Inter-Agency Standing Committee, all humanitarian actors are expected to place protection at the center of their work. In this context, protection is defined as "all activities aimed at obtaining full respect for the rights of the individual in accordance with the letter and the spirit of the relevant bodies of law."[16]

While the policy priority of protection is stated unequivocally, what protection means in practice can be vague. As was stated in a global-level evaluation of international protection interventions in 2013: "Protection defies neat labelling because it is at the same time the goal underlying the whole humanitarian response (the reason for humanitarian action), an approach or lens on the humanitarian response (a way of understanding all dimensions of humanitarian endeavour), and a more narrowly-defined family of activities that aim to prevent and mitigate threats to vulnerable persons."[17] The largely aspirational nature of the international protection framework asserts the primordial nature of rights, even as such discourse remains starkly disconnected from the realities of everyday life for those being "protected."

A general approach to protection aims to first take action to stop direct abuses, then respond to them, then offer remedial action to contribute to a more protective environment in the longer term. Yet protection responses rarely address the underlying conditions that are the cause of harm. By neglecting to deal with the profoundly complex and interlocking processes of violence, international protection interventions can sustain—and, in some cases, worsen—the very conditions they are trying to ameliorate.

In contexts such as the DRC, conditions of adversity are generalized, and most people experience deprivation. Yet international protection actions tend to be implemented through the disaggregation and categorization of the "most vulnerable." People who qualify as most vulnerable become project "beneficiaries" for the provision of aid and services—consider the rape victim or the "child soldier" described earlier. As articulated by Zoë Marriage, this process of beneficiary selection is passed off as "pragmatism" but instead "conscripts the idealism (or surrealism) that significant impact can be made with insignificant contributions."[18] By simplifying, disaggregating, and selecting, the broader structures of violence operating in the DRC are obscured, and thus can persist.

The concept of denial as elaborated by sociologist Stanley Cohen is useful in analyzing the myth of international protection in the DRC. According to Cohen, denial is that which is "known and not known at the same time."[19] It is a human capacity that allows us to consider how we cognitively deal with unwelcome truths. We know that something is wrong, and yet, without recourse to obvious better alternatives, we continue. Denial allows for international protection actors to decry and denounce the newest wave of violence, without any engagement in the overarching structures that might compel a transformation of this violence. As critiqued in other contexts, the flurry of action mobilized in response to "emergencies" simply perpetuates a "false sense that something was being done, preventing discussion and analysis around what really needed doing."[20]

## A GLOBAL POLITICAL ECONOMY OF VIOLENCE

The political and economic factors that drive the violence in the DRC are deeply connected with our global political economy. Political economy examines the relationship between the political and economic processes that underlie trade, production, and the distribution of resources. More specifically, a political economy analysis of violence examines the rationalities of violence and the benefits of war. As described by David Keen, such a perspective allows us to consider how violent conflict is "a continuation of economics by other means" and how, at times, "prolonging the war is as useful as 'winning' it."[21]

An extensive literature exists on how the contemporary wars in the DRC have been driven by competition for natural resource wealth, but even in the nineteenth century, the links between violence in the Congo Free State and economic benefits to European markets were evident. The extractive violence that laid the foundations of the Congo Free State sheds light on contemporary governance strategies.[22] In the current period, incredible wealth is being amassed by the ruling Congolese elite, while global markets continue to reap the profits of Congolese mineral resources.

Knowledge about the linkages between processes of natural resource extraction in the DRC and the ways in which global profits are connected to the perpetration of violence in the DRC is increasing, offering insights into how individual and social patterns of consumption in the global North are deeply entwined with the structures of violence in the DRC. Efforts such as the Extractive Industries Transparency Initiative (EITI) are increasing our knowledge base. In 2012, the EITI valued the extractive sector in the DRC—including tin, tantalum and tungsten (wolframite), gold, and alluvial diamonds—at US$24 trillion. These resources accounted for 99 percent of total Congolese exports and 64 percent of the government budget.[23] More recent data show that in 2014, the DRC was the leading global producer of cobalt, producing 3.4 million tons of cobalt, with an estimated 56 billion tons in store. In 2014, the DRC produced 1.1 million tons of copper, with a further 20 million tons estimated in reserve. It also produced 1.1 million carats of diamonds, more than any country in the world, and twenty-four thousand kilograms of gold.[24]

In our now globally interconnected world, we have the knowledge to see how our own patterns of consumption are intimately tied into the violence and suffering of the DRC. We can know how the tantalum/coltan, tin/cassiterite, and wolframite/tungsten that are the essential components of our mobile phones, laptops, and electric cars have been extracted from Congolese mines. Sustained attention should now be applied to understanding how cobalt is extracted in the DRC, and the pathways it takes into the lithium-ion batteries that will power our electric vehicles. It is our work as citizens to support trade policies of our governments that can facilitate support for Deaton's "great escape," including of the countless Congolese miners and families who are barely meeting their daily survival needs in some of the harshest and most dangerous physical conditions imaginable.[25]

Building on the movement to increase corporate due diligence that began with the Kimberly Process that followed the scandal of "blood" diamonds taken from the front lines of the brutal wars in Sierra Leone and Liberia at the beginning of the twenty-first century, as consumers we can insist on ever greater transparency and accountability by corporations that are involved in natural resource extraction in conflict zones. Such processes are not without unintended negative consequences; these range from penalizing the poorest, artisanal miner to pushing out legitimate companies that are simply replaced by ones less concerned about "due diligence." Yet they represent an important societal and political shift that acknowledges how patterns of consumption among the wealthy are fueling violence and contributing to entrenched hardship throughout the world.

Less clearly elucidated—but undeniable—are the ways in which the international aid system operates in this global political economy, and here much greater analytical attention is needed. As documented by Hochschild, the intentions of the devoted Western humanitarians of the nineteenth century offer one starting place for increased reflexivity on the power and positionality of those engaging to "do good": "Europeans liked to think of themselves as having higher motives. The British, in particular, fervently believed in bringing 'civilization' and Christianity to the natives; they were curious about what lay in the continent's unknown interior; and they were filled with righteousness about combating slavery."[26] This colonial-era ardor was of *une mission civilisatrice*—or the will to "improve" people living in faraway lands.[27] Today such endeavors have been transposed into agnostic tropes like "capacity building" and "good governance," goals that coalesce nicely with global neoliberal economic priorities. Such goals have notably brought great wealth to a small minority of the world's population, at the expense of the world's greater majority.

## RESISTING CYNICAL REASON

In his foreword to Peter Sloterdijk's *Critique of Cynical Reason*, Andreas Huyssen refers to Immanuel Kant's inquiry: "What's going on right now? What's happening to us? What is this world, this period, this precise moment in which we are living?"[28] This Kantian inquiry, dated 1784, still resonates, still urges us to remain engaged, to shun complacency, to act in our world in ways that might one day at last ensure "the inherent dignity" and respect "of the equal and inalienable rights of all members of the human family."[29]

Such idealism can be difficult to sustain in a period when millions of people are dying in man-made crises. Worldwide, violent conflict continues to kill an estimated seventy thousand people each year, while nonconflict violent deaths, mostly by firearms, surpass more than five hundred thousand annually.[30] Seventy years after the enactment of the Universal Declaration of Human Rights, hundreds of thousands of people are dying in wars that are not inevitable. Many millions are being pushed from their homes, fearful, hungry, and struggling to survive each day. We are very far away from the protections and assurance of human dignity the UN has mandated itself to ensure.

This is true not only in the global South but also in the wealthiest economies of the world.[31] In a period of rising fear and populist national politics, the catastrophic hatreds of the early twentieth century seem not so far away. They are being echoed in the political vitriol of leaders who mobilize people's fears about rising precarity and economic insecurity. This is as true today in France, where I have made my home and where my son is growing up, as in the many villages I visited in the DRC over the years.

In such a political climate of fear, idealism begins to feel like a form of personal political resistance that is, ironically, not so far from Sloterdijk's modern-day cynic. For him, working to expose the moral scandals of our time requires "a stance of extreme closeness."[32] Yet this closeness is what feels most threatening to the many people who are falling off the edges of the world's ever more exclusive havens of prosperity. Many see threats to their own existence embodied in the migrants escaping the worst of human brutality and injustice in search of even the possibility of human dignity.

At the same time, closeness is that which confronts us with the inescapability of our shared humanity. In my study of violence, so frequently confronted by the bleakness of it all, I often turn to Buddhist scholar Pema Chödrön to try to make sense of our dark human depths. Her teaching on compassion helps me: "Compassion is not a relationship between the healer and the wounded. It's a relationship between equals. Only when we know our own darkness well can we be present with the darkness of others."[33]

More than anywhere else, in the DRC I became aware of how raw, uncertain, and troubling a sense of equality and knowledge of our shared humanity can feel. One of so many revelatory moments occurred one afternoon in 2009, when I was interviewing a demobilized FDLR element in the Mutobo camp in Rwanda, part of an investigation to establish chain of command and thus responsibility for a series of horrific atrocities that had occurred in the DRC. I went into the interview laden with my presumptions, supported by the weight of a UN mandate. According to most, this man was an enemy. A terrorist. Yet the more I listened to his words, the more clearly I could hear what he was saying. His jaw had been blown out by a grenade, and his face was severely disfigured. But it was not pity that removed his "enemy" shroud from my eyes. His voice shook at first, but over time it resonated. He told a deeply human, achingly painful story. A story of loss, fear, and suffering. A story of violence inherited and then transmitted.

I thought of this man again a few months ago, just one of the countless moments when I am surprised by how much the DRC remains in me, transposed yet present. My son and I were leaving his school after the main doors had already closed for the day. In the courtyard, we heard an alarm being tested. I wondered aloud if it was the fire alarm, but my son replied:

No, Mama, it's the alarm for when the *méchants* come to school.
   The bad ones? Which bad ones?
   The very bad ones. When that alarm goes off, we have to be silent, and then find our way to hide in the dark.

I was stunned. First, because as a parent, I should have been told about this kind of school drill in response to a "terrorist" attack but had not been. Second, because the narrative of good and bad had been appropriated before I had had the time to think sufficiently through how I would want to guide my child through such times of darkness. France, like so many other states today, is trying to deal with the threats posed to its internal security, as it must. But if I apply the knowledge about humanity offered to me by the DRC, I know that addressing violence and hatred through fear and more violence only conserves violence.

The conservation of violence is not inevitable. In her work on how the Brazilian art of capoeira has historically served to resist entrenched violence and inequality, Zoë Marriage questions the often-assumed inevitability of violence.[34] She considers how violence can be resisted and transformed. This requires a revolution in approach, a view of "resistance as a way of life, resisting not so much through confrontation but by making strange and proposing alternative outcomes to historically entrenched inequality."[35] The violence that continues to plague our world is at once deeply political and intimately personal. As taught by Shantideva more than a millennium ago, we must come to know how our individual actions are neither independent nor autonomous from this violence.[36] How we choose to transform it—or not—is in the actions of our everyday.

# NOTES

## CHAPTER ONE. A BEGINNING

1. Benjamin Coghlan et al. (2006) published an article in the *Lancet* that estimated five million deaths. This figure has been contested; see Human Security Report Project 2010; Muggah 2011.

2. The UN peacekeeping mission has been present in the eastern DRC since 1999, with around twenty thousand military peacekeepers and police and three thousand civilians.

3. This is the title of Gérard Prunier's 2009 account of the 1996–97 and 1998–2003 wars that drew in nine countries to fight on Congolese soil.

4. To protect the individuals mentioned in this book, pseudonyms have been used throughout, in all but one case—that of the artist whose artwork and narratives are featured in chapter 4.

5. Keen 1997, p. 68.

6. The embodiment of violence is a subject treated by Philippe Bourgois in his ethnographic work that traces the lines between the Salvadoran civil war of the early 1980s to the crack-ravaged streets of present-day East Harlem. As he noted, "People do not simply 'survive' violence as if it somehow remained outside of them"; rather, it becomes incorporated in their way in being in and perceiving the world (Bourgois 2001, p. 29).

7. As mandated by UN Security Council Resolution 1857; see United Nations 2009.

8. See, e.g., Hart and Tyrer 2006. Jason Hart would become a key influence on my work and eventually served as my external PhD examiner.

9. As a child protection adviser with the Mission de l'Organisation des Nations Unies en République démocratique du Congo (MONUC), I interviewed more than 300 young people separated from armed groups, plus at least another 200 parents, community leaders, and authorities. With the UN Group of Experts, I conducted interviews with various actors involved in the conflict, as well as with 80 young people separated from armed groups, 40 elements of the Forces démocratiques de libération du Rwanda (FDLR), and more than 150 people who had been displaced by violence or had witnessed grave human rights violations. During the research consultancies I conducted for War Child Holland and War Child UK, I interviewed approximately 500 children and adults. With Save the Children UK, I interviewed or convened focus group discussions with more than 600 people. With Oxfam GB, I interviewed an additional 30 UN and NGO workers on behalf of the DRC Protection Cluster. With the Small Arms Survey I interviewed approximately 50 researchers, and with the USAID-ECCN network I consulted with an additional 40 individuals.

10. Many of the analyses and narratives included in this book have already been published in other articles and edited volumes. See Seymour 2011a, 2011b, 2012, 2013, 2014a, 2014b, 2017a, 2017b. I am grateful to Save the Children UK, War Child Holland, and War Child UK for their willingness to contribute to this research.

11. Bourdieu describes the law of conservation of violence as "the inclination to violence that is engendered by early and constant exposure to violence" (2000, p. 233).

12. The notion of making explicit comes from Bourdieu 2000, p. 188.

13. Chapter 4 includes an in-depth critique of international responses to militarized sexual violence in the DRC. For an examination of the international processes around the mining sector, see Seay 2012; Wolfe 2015; Verweijin 2017.

14. For more on the California Series in Public Anthropology, see www.publicanthropology.org/books-book-series/california-book-series/.

15. See Wessells 2009 for a sensitive treatment of the "do no harm" challenges facing psychosocial workers in contemporary zones of conflict.

16. David Keen, in his political economy analysis of famine, *The Benefits of Famine: A Political Economy of Famine and Relief in Southwestern Sudan, 1983–1989* (1994), draws on Michel Foucault's study of Stalin's gulags and questions how famine and its humanitarian response have economic beneficiaries.

## CHAPTER TWO. OUTRAGES IN CONGO

1. Lorraine Macmillan (2009) presents a compelling critique of international responses to the "child soldier" phenomenon.

2. See, e.g., Kaldor 2013.

3. See IRIN 2009.

4. In 2005, UN Security Council Resolution 1612 established the Monitoring and Reporting Mechanism to monitor and report on six grave violations of children's rights in conflict-affected contexts. One of the six grave violations was the recruitment and use of children by armed forces or armed groups. The six grave child rights violations include killing or maiming; recruiting or using child soldiers; attacks against schools or hospitals; rape or other grave sexual violence; abduction; and denial of humanitarian access. https://childrenandarmedconflict.un.org/our-work/monitoring-and-reporting/.

5. The 1997 Cape Town Principles and Best Practices on the prevention of recruitment of children into the armed forces and on demobilizaton and social reintegration of child soldiers in Africa were followed in 2007 by the Paris Principles, or the Principles and Guidelines on Children Associated with Armed Forces and Armed Groups; see https://childrenandarmedconflict.un.org/publications/ParisPrinciples_EN.pdf.

6. Rome Statute, Article 8, b (xxvi). Earlier international instruments laid the foundations for an international norm that sets eighteen years as the minimum age for lawful recruitment into nonstate armed

groups; see the Convention on the Rights of the Child, its Optional Protocol on the Involvement of Children in Armed Conflict, the African Charter on the Rights and Welfare of the Child, and the ILO Convention concerning the Prohibition and Immediate Action for the Elimination of the Worst Forms of Child Labour.

7. As described in the Paris Principles, Article 2.8, p. 7; https://www.unicef.org/emerg/files/ParisPrinciples310107English.pdf.

8. Interview, Bukavu, April 2010.

9. Group discussion, Goma, July 2010.

10. Prunier 2009, p. 251.

11. Interview, Bunyakiri, May 2010.

12. Group discussion, Bunyakiri, May 2010.

13. Group discussion, Bunyakiri, June 2010.

14. The concept of "founding violence" is elaborated by Veena Das (2007), who considers how the violence that lays the foundations of state creation (in her research, the Indian subcontinent) continues to reverberate decades later.

15. Full contents of letter available at http://www.blackpast.org/george-washington-williams-open-letter-king-leopold-congo-1890#sthash.LpogtRHT.JikXvgoN.dpuf, citing source as Adelaide Cromwell Hill and Martin Kilson, eds., *Apropos of Africa: Sentiments of American Negro Leaders on Africa from the 1800s to the 1950s* (London: Frank Cass, 1969).

16. Ibid.

17. Hochschild 1998.

18. See Pottier 2002; Jackson 2007. This pattern continues today, with between one and two million people reported to be displaced in the region at any given time.

19. See Mararo 1997; Mamdani 2002; Jackson 2007; Raeymaekers 2010.

20. Nzongola-Ntalaja 2002.

21. Pottier 2002.

22. Over the years, the dynamics of the conflict in relation to the ex-FAR/ALiR/FDLR changed significantly. While the AFDL fought against the ex-FAR/ALiR in alliance with the RPF during the 1996–97 phase of the war, the split of the alliance in 1998 led to Laurent Kabila's intermittent joining of forces with the ALiR/FDLR against the RPF

in the second phase of the war. Over the years, FDLR elements were integrated into local society, married Congolese women, and recruited Congolese nationals. Although they established strong control over key mining and trade routes and often operated brutal local taxation rackets, the FDLR were mostly tolerated by the local population.

23. Prunier 2009.

24. The purported assistance of the Rwandan government considerably strengthened the CNDP's military advantage.

25. While some commanders of the FARDC continued to cooperate with the FDLR in operations against other armed groups, the FDLR also benefited from remittances of Rwandans who had emigrated, as well as on local income generation from gold and tin ore, trade, agriculture, fishing and poaching, and marijuana trade; see Debelle and Florquin 2015.

26. United Nations 2009.

27. Human Rights Watch 2009, p. 10.

28. *News of Rwanda* 2012.

29. Vlassenroot 2013, p. 8.

30. According to a report by Jason Stearns and Christoph Vogel (2015), in 2015 there were seventy armed groups estimated to be active in the provinces of the Kivus alone.

31. Bourdieu 2000, p. 233.

32. Interview, Bunyakiri, April 2010.

33. Group discussion, Bukavu, May 2010.

34. Group discussion, Mushinga, April 2010.

35. Ibid.

36. Interview, Goma, May 2009.

37. Interview, Bunyakiri, May 2010.

38. Interview, Bunyakiri, June 2010.

39. Interview, Mushinga, April 2010.

## CHAPTER THREE. SURVIVING VIOLENCE

1. Miller and Rasmussen 2010, p. 10.

2. *Oxford Concise Medical Dictionary*, 2002.

3. American Psychiatric Association 2000.

4. For an extensive review of the literature, see Seymour 2013.

5. Garbarino and Kostelny 1996, pp. 33–34.

6. Ladd and Cairns 1996, p. 14.

7. Summerfield 1997, p. 1568.

8. See the work of Michael Wessells (2009). Other research in Sri Lanka, the West Bank, and Chad showed that the correlation between war experience and the expression of PTSD symptoms was much less significant than what previous research had shown; see Fernando, Miller, and Berger 2010; Al-Krenawi, Lev-Wiesel, and Sehwail 2007; Rasmussen et al. 2010.

9. Garbarino and Kostelny 1996, p. 33; Ladd and Cairns 1996, p. 14.

10. For an extensive review of the literature, see Seymour 2013.

11. Rutter 2000, p. 653. The term "resilience" is borrowed from the field of epidemiology, where it is defined as "the factors that accentuate or inhibit disease and deficiency states, and the processes that underlie them"; see Haggerty et al. 1994, p. 9.

12. Masten 2001, p. 227.

13. Ungar 2008, p. 225.

14. Group discussion, Bukavu, April 2010.

15. Galtung 1969, p. 173.

16. Group discussion, Bukavu, June 2010.

17. Farmer 2004, p. 309.

18. Interview, Bunyakiri, May 2010.

19. Group discussion, Bunyakiri, April 2010.

20. Interview, Goma, February 2009.

21. Group discussion, Goma, June 2011.

22. Group discussion, Bukavu, April 2010.

23. Group discussion, Bukavu, June 2010.

24. Group discussion, Bunyakiri, April 2010.

25. Group discussion, Bukavu, April 2010.

26. Interview, Bunyakiri, June 2010.

27. Group discussion, Bukavu, May 2010.

28. Interview, Goma, June 2011.

### CHAPTER FOUR. EMBODYING VIOLENCE

1. Hilhorst and Douma 2018; Eriksson Baaz and Stern 2013.

2. In June 2014, the Global Summit to End Sexual Violence in Conflict was chaired by then-UK foreign secretary William Hague and Hollywood star Angelina Jolie. According to the summit organizers: "This was the largest gathering ever brought together on the subject [of sexual violence in conflict], with 1,700 delegates and 123 country delegations including 79 Ministers.... During the Summit there were over 175 public events in London, and an 84-hour global relay of events around the world." https://www.gov.uk/government/topical-events/sexual-violence-in-conflict. According to the *Guardian,* the summit cost more than 5 million pounds; see Mark Townsend, "William Hague's Summit against Warzone Rape Seen as 'Costly Failure,'" *Guardian,* 13 June 2015, https://www.theguardian.com/global-development/2015/jun/13/warzone-rape-congo-questions-uk-campaign.

3. BBC 2010.

4. Human Rights Watch 2014.

5. United Nations 2010, p. 8.

6. MacFarquhar 2010.

7. Interview with director of local NGO in Bukavu, February 2010.

8. Eriksson Baaz and Stern 2013, p. 11.

9. Eriksson Baaz and Stern 2010, p. 13.

10. Hilhorst and Douma 2018, p. S95.

11. Interview, Bukavu, April 2010.

12. Kleinman 2000.

13. Multiple group discussions, South Kivu, May–July 2010.

14. Group discussion, Bunyakri, June 2010.

15. Lwambo 2011.

16. Hunter 2002.

17. Interview, Goma, July 2010.

18. Interview, Goma, July 2010.

19. Interview, Bukavu, January 2010.

20. Robinson and Yeh 2011, pp. 1–2.

21. Group discussion, girls fourteen to seventeen years old, Goma, July 2011.

22. Interview, Nyakariba, July 2011.

23. Group discussion with parents, Butembo, August 2011.

24. Multiple interviews, Goma, July 2010.

25. Group discussion, Goma, July 2010.
26. Doris Schopper (2014) has examined the evidence on the impact of sexual violence response programs. Despite massive international investments and the emergence of a strong normative framework, we still know very little about the effectiveness of such interventions.

### CHAPTER FIVE. NAVIGATING VIOLENCE

1. Interview, Bunyakiri, May 2010.
2. Group discussion, Bukavu, April 2010.
3. Bandura 2001, p. 10.
4. de Certeau 1984, p. 30.
5. Honwana 2001; Utas 2005.
6. See Olivier de Sardan 1996 for a detailed treatment of this concept.
7. Larousse Online Dictionary, n.d., http://www.larousse.com/en/dictionnaires/francais/se_d%C3%A9brouiller/21929.
8. According to Eriksson Baaz and Stern (2010, p. 35): "The meaning of *la débrouillardise* comes from the legitimating of the illegal practice of artisan diamond digging after the secession of South Kasai in the 1960s. Since the state lacked a budget, its leader, Albert Kalondji, decreed *'débrouillez-vous'* to be Article 15 of the constitution of the territory of the Luba-Kasai ... thus liberalizing the diamond industry.... This simple *'débrouillez-vous'* order was subsequently given to the whole nation by President Mobutu, and has since become associated with all illegal activities: corruption, theft, smuggling, embezzlement."
9. MacGaffey 1986, p. 141.
10. Group discussion, Bunyakiri, May 2010.
11. Interview, Goma, July 2010
12. Interview on behalf of War Child UK, Goma, July 2010.
13. Interview, Bukavu, January 2010.
14. Group discussion, Bukavu, July 2010.
15. Interview, Masisi Territory, June 2011.
16. Group discussion with parents, Nyakariba, July 2011.
17. Group discussion with parents, Lubero, August 2011.
18. Group discussion with parents, Butembo, August 2011.

19. Group discussion with parents, Lubero, August 2011.

20. Group discussion, Butembo, August 2011.

21. Interview, Goma, July 2011.

22. Boothby, Strang, and Wessells 2006.

23. Group discussion with parents, Boga, August 2011.

24. Group discussion with parents, Boga, August 2011.

25. Interview, Masisi town, July 2011.

26. Group discussion, Boga, June 2011.

27. Scott 1972, p. 92.

28. Ibid., p. 102.

29. Vlassenroot 2000a.

30. Mamdani 2002.

31. Chabal 2009, p. 89.

32. Young 1965, p. 72; Prunier 2009, p. 49.

33. Young 1965, pp. 59, 72.

34. Vlassenroot and Romkema 2007, p. 9.

35. Vigh 2006, p. 124.

36. de Waal 2009, p. 13.

37. Vlassenroot and Romkema 2007.

38. For "retreat from citizens," see Reno 1998, p. 153.

39. Olivier de Sardan 1999, p. 46.

40. Prunier 2009, p. 278.

41. Young, as cited in Lemarchand 1972, p. 69.

42. Reno 1998, p. 158.

43. Ibid.

44. Trefon 2004.

45. Nzeza Bilakila 2004, p. 23.

46. Vlassenroot and Romkema 2007, p. 19.

47. For early theoretical treatment of the dependency complex, see Mannoni 1950.

48. McLean 2005, p. 650.

49. Ibid., p. 639.

50. Group discussion, Bukavu, April 2010.

51. Interview, Bukavu, April 2010.

52. Utas 2005, p. 403.

53. Marriage 2012.

CHAPTER SIX. MEANINGS OF VIOLENCE

1. Rutter 2000, p. 674.
2. Heine, Proulx, and Vohs 2006, p. 89.
3. Frankl (1959) 2006.
4. Wessells and Strang 2006.
5. Chabal and Daloz 1999, p. 56.
6. Group discussion, Mushinga, April 2010.
7. Vlassenroot 2000b.
8. Interview, Mushinga, May 2010.
9. Interview, Masisi Territory, July 2011.
10. Arendt 1969.
11. Group discussion, Bukavu, May 2010.
12. Lazarus and Launier 1978.
13. Macleod 1987, p. 8.
14. Ibid., p. 112.
15. Bourgois 2003.
16. Interview, Bukavu, May 2010.
17. Interview, Mushinga, May 2010.
18. Interview, Bunyakiri, April 2010.
19. Kleinman 2000, p. 227.
20. Interview, Bunyakiri, July 2010.
21. Interview, Bunyakiri, May 2010.
22. Interview, Lubero, August 2011.
23. Lumumba's killing remains shrouded in speculation, although it is widely believed to have been orchestrated by Western intelligence services.
24. Patrice Lumumba, first prime minister of the Congo, 30 June 1960, Independence Day, http://www.friendsofthecongo.org/speeches .html.
25. Interview, Goma, July 2009.
26. Fanon (1961) 1967, p. 27.
27. For more about LUCHA, see http://www.luchacongo.org/.
28. Amnesty International, https://www.amnesty.org/en/latest /news/2016/07/drc-release-of-six-youth-activists-must-lead-to-freedom -for-all-prisoners-of-conscience/.

## CHAPTER SEVEN. THE MYTH OF INTERNATIONAL PROTECTION

1. DFID 2014, p. 5.

2. See the OCHA press release "The Single Largest Impediment to the Humanitarian Response in the DRC Is Underfunding"; http://www.unocha.org//story/single-largest-impediment-humanitarian-response-drc-underfunding-un-humanitarian-chief.

3. AFP 2017.

4. BBC 2017.

5. UN OCHA 2017a.

6. Channel Research 2011.

7. UN OCHA 2017c.

8. UN OCHA 2017b.

9. Deaton 2013, p. 294.

10. Duffield 2005, p. 156.

11. CHS Alliance, Group URD and the Sphere Project 2014.

12. Duffield 2007, p. viii.

13. Group discussion, Bunyakiri, April 2010.

14. Roy 2010, p. 85.

15. For more information, see http://www.un.org/en/genocideprevention/about-responsibility-to-protect.html.

16. IASC (Inter-Agency Standing Committee) 2013.

17. Murray and Landry 2013, p. 4.

18. Marriage 2006, p. 225.

19. Cohen 2001, p. 79.

20. Levine and Chastre 2004, p. 19.

21. Keen 1997, p. 69. In his political economy analysis of famine in the Horn of Africa in the late 1980s, David Keen questions how famine was promoted by some actors for rational and beneficial ends; see also Keen 1994.

22. As noted by Charles Tilly (1985, p. 169): "At least for the European experience of the past few centuries, a portrait of war makers and state makers as coercive and self-seeking entrepreneurs bears a far greater resemblance to the facts than do its chief alternatives."

23. EITI 2012.

24. For details, see https://eiti.org/democratic-republic-of-congo.

25. Frankel 2016.

26. Hochschild 1998, p. 27.

27. Paris 2002, p. 651.

28. Huyssen 1988, p. xi.

29. United Nations 1948.

30. GBAV 2015.

31. The UN Special Rapporteur on extreme poverty and human rights conducted an investigation in the United States in 2017; his findings can be read at https://www.theguardian.com/world/2017/dec/15/extreme-poverty-america-un-special-monitor-report.

32. Sloterdijk 1988, p. xxxii.

33. Chödrön 2002.

34. Marriage 2017.

35. Ibid., p. 16.

36. Shantideva, as quoted in Chödrön 2007.

# REFERENCES

AFP. 2017. "400,000 Children in DR Congo Could Die from Hunger, Says Unicef." https://www.afp.com/en/news/23/400000-children -dr-congo-could-die-hunger-says-unicef-doc-v33xz1.

Al-Krenawi, Alean, Rachel Lev-Wiesel, and Mahmud Sehwail. 2007. "Psychological Symptomatology among Palestinian Children Living with Political Violence." *Child and Adolescent Mental Health* 12:27–31.

American Psychiatric Association. 2000. *Diagnostic and Statistical Manual of Mental Disorders.* 4th ed. Washington, DC: American Psychiatric Association.

Arendt, Hannah. 1969. "Reflections on Violence." In *Anthology: Selected Essays from the First 30 Years of* The New York Review of Books, 33–76. New York: New York Review of Books.

Association of Social Anthropologists. 2011. *Ethical Guidelines for Good Research Practice.* Association of Social Anthropologists of the UK and the Commonwealth.

Bandura, Albert. 2001. "Social Cognitive Theory: An Agentic Perspective." *Annual Review of Psychology* 52:1–26.

BBC (British Broadcasting Corporation). 2010. "UN Official Calls DR Congo 'Rape Capital of the World.'" BBC, 28 April. http://news .bbc.co.uk/2/hi/8650112.stm.

————. 2017. "Hunger Road." BBC, 12 December. http://www.bbc
.com/news/av/world-africa-42333743/
dr-congo-crisis-on-kasai-s-hunger-road.

Boothby, Neil, Alison Strang, and Michael Wessells. 2006. Introduction. In *A World Turned Upside Down: Social Ecological Approaches to Children in War Zones*, edited by N. Boothby, A. Strang, and M. Wessells, 1–18. Bloomfield, CT: Kumarian Press.

Bourdieu, Pierre. 2000. *Pascalian Meditations*. Stanford, CA: Stanford University Press.

Bourgois, Philippe. 2001. "The Power of Violence in War and Peace: Post–Cold War Lessons from El Salvador." *Ethnography* 2 (1): 5–34.

————. 2003. *In Search of Respect: Selling Crack in El Barrio*. Cambridge: Cambridge University Press.

Chabal, Patrick. 2009. *Africa: The Politics of Suffering and Smiling*. London: Zed Books.

Chabal, Patrick, and Jean-Pascal Daloz. 1999. *Africa Works. The Political Instrumentalization of Disorder*. Bloomington: International African Institute in association with James Currey and Indiana University Press.

Channel Research. 2011. *Joint Evaluation of Conflict Prevention and Peace-Building in the Democratic Republic of Congo*. https://www.oecd.org/countries/congo/48859543.pdf.

Chödrön, Pema. 2002. *The Places That Scare You: A Guide to Fearlessness in Difficult Times*. Boston: Shambala Publications.

————. 2007. *No Time to Lose: A Timely Guide to the Way of the Bodhisattva*. Boston: Shambala Publications.

CHS Alliance, Group URD, and the Sphere Project. 2014. "Core Humanitarian Standard on Quality and Accountability." https://corehumanitarianstandard.org/files/files/Core%20Humanitarian%20Standard%20-%20English.pdf.

Coghlan, Benjamin, Richard J. Brennan, Pascal Ngoy, David Dofara, Brad Otto, Mark Clements, and Tony Stewart. 2006. "Mortality in the Democratic Republic of Congo: A Nationwide Survey." *Lancet* 367:44–51.

Cohen, Stanley. 2001. *States of Denial: Knowing about Atrocities and Suffering*. Cambridge: Polity Press.

Das, Veena. 2007. *Life and Words: Violence and the Descent into the Ordinary.* Berkeley: University of California Press.

Deaton, Angus. 2013. *The Great Escape: Health, Wealth, and the Origins of Inequality.* Princeton, NJ: Princeton University Press.

Debelle, Raymond, and Nicolas Florquin. 2015. "Waning Cohesion: The Rise and Fall of the FDLR." In *Small Arms Survey 2015: Weapons and the World*, edited by Small Arms Survey, 186–98. Cambridge: Cambridge University Press.

De Certeau, Michel. 1984. *The Practice of Everyday Life.* Berkeley: University of California Press.

de Waal, Alex. 2009. "Fixing the Political Marketplace: How Can We Make Peace without Functioning State Institutions?" Bergen, Norway: Chr Michelsen Institute.

DFID (Department for International Development). 2014. "2011–2016 Operational Plan, Updated in December 2014." https://www.gov.uk/government/uploads/system/uploads/attachment_data/file/38 9482/DRC_Operational_Plan.pdf.

Duffield, Mark. 2005. "Getting Savages to Fight Barbarians: Development, Security and the Colonial Present." *Conflict, Security and Development* 5 (2): 141–59.

————. 2007. *Development, Security and Unending War: Governing the World of Peoples.* Cambridge: Polity Press.

EITI (Extractive Industries Transparency Initiative). 2012. "Executive Committee of the Extractive Industries Transparency Initiative Reconciliation Report for the Year 2012, December 2014."

Eriksson Baaz, Maria, and Maria Stern. 2010. *The Complexity of Violence: A Critical Analysis of Sexual Violence in the Democratic Republic of Congo.* Uppsala: Nordiska Afrikainstitutet.

————. 2013. *Sexual Violence as a Weapon of War? Perceptions, Prescriptions, Problems in the Congo and Beyond.* London: Zed Books.

Fanon, Franz. (1961) 1967. *The Wretched of the Earth.* London: Penguin Books.

Farmer, Paul. 2004. "An Anthropology of Structural Violence." *Current Anthropology* 45 (3): 305–25.

Fernando, Gaithri, Kenneth Miller, and Dale Berger. 2010. "Growing Pains: The Impact of Disaster-Related and Daily Stressors on the

Psychological and Psychosocial Functioning of Youth in Sri Lanka." *Child Development* 81 (4): 1192–210.

Frankel, Todd C. 2016. "The Cobalt Pipeline: Tracing the Path from Deadly Hand-Dug Mines in Congo to Consumers' Phones and Laptops." *Washington Post*, 30 September. https://www.washington post.com/graphics/business/batteries/congo-cobalt-mining-for-lit hium-ion-battery/.

Frankl, Viktor. (1959) 2006. *Man's Search for Meaning.* Boston: Beacon Press.

Galtung, Johan. 1969. "Violence, Peace and Peace Research." *Journal of Peace Research* 6 (3): 167–91.

Garbarino, James, and Kathleen Kostelny. 1996. "The Effects of Political Violence on Palestinian Children's Behavior Problems: A Risk Accumulation Model." *Child Development* 67 (1): 33–45.

GBAV (Global Burden of Armed Violence). 2015. *Global Burden of Armed Violence 2015: Every Body Counts.* Geneva: Small Arms Survey.

Haggerty, Robert J., Lonnie R. Sherrod, Norman Garmezy, and Michael Rutter, eds. 1994. *Stress, Risk, and Resilience in Children and Adolescents: Processes, Mechanisms, and Interventions.* Cambridge: Cambridge University Press.

Hart, Jason, and Bex Tyrer. 2006. "Research with Children Living in Situations of Armed Conflict: Concepts, Ethics and Methods." Refugee Studies Centre Working Paper Series, 30.

Heine, Steven, Travis Proulx, and Kathleen Vohs. 2006. "The Meaning Maintenance Model: On the Coherence of Social Motivations." *Personality and Social Psychology Review* 10 (2): 88–110.

Hilhorst, Dorothea, and Nynke Douma. 2018. "Beyond the Hype? The Response to Sexual Violence in the Democratic Republic of the Congo in 2011 and 2014." *Disasters* 42 (S1): S79–S98.

Hochschild, Adam. 1998. *King Leopold's Ghost: A Story of Greed, Terror, and Heroism in Colonial Africa.* Boston: Houghton Mifflin.

Honwana, Alcinda. 2001. "Children of War: Local Understandings of War and War Trauma in Mozambique and Angola." In *Civilians at War,* edited by S. Chesterman, 123–44. Boulder, CO: Lynne Rienner.

Human Rights Watch. 2009. "You Will Be Punished: Attacks on Civilians in Eastern Congo." https://www.hrw.org/report/2009/12/13 /you-will-be-punished/attacks-civilians-eastern-congo.

———. 2014. "Democratic Republic of Congo: Ending Impunity for Sexual Violence." https://www.hrw.org/news/2014/06/10/democra tic-republic-congo-ending-impunity-sexual-violence.

Human Security Report Project. 2010. *Human Security Report 2009: The Shrinking Costs of War.* Oxford: Oxford University Press.

Hunter, Mark. 2002. "The Materiality of Everyday Sex: Thinking beyond Prostitution." *African Studies* 61 (1): 99–120.

Huyssen, Andreas. 1988. "Foreword." In Peter Sloterdijk, *Critique of Cynical Reason*, ix–xxv. Minneapolis: University of Minnesota Press.

IASC (Inter-Agency Standing Committee). 2013. "The Centrality of Protection in Humanitarian Action Statement by the Inter-Agency Standing Committee Principles."

IRIN (Integrated Regional Information Networks). 2009. "In Brief: DRC Child Recruitment a 'Tragic Consequence' of War." 1 September. http://www.irinnews.org/report/85945/brief-drc-child-re cruitment-tragic-consequence-war.

Jackson, Stephen. 2007. "Of 'Doubtful Nationality': Political Manipulation of Citizenship in the D.R. Congo." *Citizenship Studies* 11 (5): 481–500.

Kaldor, Mary. 2013. "In Defence of New Wars." *Stability: International Journal of Security and Development* 2 (1): 1–16.

Keen, David. 1994. *The Benefits of Famine: A Political Economy of Famine and Relief in Southwestern Sudan, 1983–1989.* Princeton, NJ: Princeton University Press.

———. 1997. "A Rational Kind of Madness." *Oxford Development Studies* 25 (1): 67–75.

Kleinman, Arthur. 2000. "The Violences of Everyday Life: The Multiple Forms and Dynamics of Social Violence." In *Violence and Subjectivity*, edited by V. Das, A. Kleinman, M. Ramphele, and P. Reynolds, 226–41. Berkeley: University of California Press.

Ladd, Gary, and Ed Cairns. 1996. "Children: Ethnic and Political Violence." *Child Development* 67 (1): 14–18.

Lazarus, Richard, and Raymond Launier. 1978. "Stress-Related Transactions between Person and Environment." In *Perspectives in Interactional Psychology*, edited by L.A. Pervin and M. Lewis, 287–327. New York: Plenum Press.

Lemarchand, Réne. 1972. "Political Clientelism and Ethnicity in Tropical Africa: Competing Solidarities in Nation-Building." *American Political Science Review* 66 (1): 68–90.

Levine, Simon, and Claire Chastre. 2004. *Missing the Point: An Analysis of Food Security Interventions in the Great Lakes.* London: Overseas Development Institute.

Lwambo, Desirée. 2011. "'Before the War, I Was a Man': Men and Masculinities in Eastern DR Congo." http://www.healafrica.org /wp-content/uploads/2011/10/men-and-masculinities-in-eastern-dr -congo.pdf.

MacFarquhar, Neil. 2010. "U.N. Says about 500 Were Raped in Congo." *New York Times,* 7 September, A8.

MacGaffey, Janet. 1986. "Fending-for-Yourself: The Organization of the Second Economy in Zaire." In *The Crisis in Zaire: Myths and Realities,* edited by G. Nzongola-Ntalaja, 141–56. Trenton, NJ: Africa World Press.

MacLeod, Jay. 1987. *Ain't No Makin' It: Leveled Aspirations in a Low-Income Neighborhood.* Boulder, CO: Westview Press.

Macmillan, Lorraine. 2009. "The Child Soldier in North-South Relations." *International Political Sociology* 3 (1): 36–52.

Mamdani, Mahmood. 2002. *When Victims Become Killers: Colonialism, Nativism, and the Genocide in Rwanda.* Princeton, NJ: Princeton University Press.

Mannoni, Dominique-Octave. 1950. *Psychologie de la Colonisation.* Paris: Éditions du Seuil.

Mararo, Bucyalimwe. 1997. "Land, Power, and Ethnic Conflict in Masisi (Congo-Kinshasa), 1940s–1994." *International Journal of African Historical Studies* 30 (3): 503–38.

Marriage, Zoë. 2006. *Not Breaking the Rules Not Playing the Game: International Assistance to Countries at War.* London: Hurst.

————. 2012. "Tactics!" *Capoeira and Security,* weblog post, 22 June. http://capoeira-security.blogspot.com.

————. 2017. "Evading Biopolitical Control: Capoeira as Total Resistance." *Global Society* 32 (3): 263–80.

Masten, Ann. 2001. "Ordinary Magic: Resilience Processes in Development." *American Psychologist* 56 (3): 227–38.

McLean, Paul. 2005. "Patronage, Citizenship, and the Stalled Emergence of the Modern State in Renaissance Florence." *Comparative Studies in Society and History* 47 (3): 638–64.

Miller, Kenneth, and Andrew Rasmussen. 2010. "War Exposure, Daily Stressors, and Mental Health in Conflict and Post-conflict Settings: Bridging the Divide between Trauma-Focused and Psychosocial Frameworks." *Social Science and Medicine* 70 (1): 7–16.

Muggah, Robert. 2011. "Measuring the True Costs of War: Consensus and Controversy." *PLoS Med* 8 (2): e1000417.

Murray, Julien, and Joseph Landry. 2013. "Placing Protection at the Centre of Humanitarian Action: Study on Protection Funding in Complex Humanitarian Emergencies." http://www.globalprotec tioncluster.org/_assets/files/news_and_publications/GPC_fund ing_study_online_EN.pdf.

*News of Rwanda.* 2012. "Rwanda: Is There Any Alternative to Eastern Congo's Conflict?" 1 August. http://newsofrwanda.com/irembo /11732/rwanda-alternative-eastern-congos-conflict/.

Nzeza Bilakila, Anastase. 2004. "The Kinshasa Bargain." In *Reinventing Order in the Congo: How People Respond to State Failure in Kinshasa,* edited by T. Trefon, 20–32. London and Kampala: Zed Books and Fountain Publishers.

Nzongola-Ntalaja, Georges. 2002. *The Congo from Leopold to Kabila: A People's History.* London: Zed Books.

Olivier de Sardan, Jean-Pierre. 1996. "L'économie morale de la corruption en Afrique." *Politique africaine* 63:97–116.

———. 1999. "A Moral Economy of Corruption in Africa?" *Journal of Modern African Studies* 37 (1): 25–52.

Paris, Roland. 2002. "International Peacebuilding and the 'Mission Civilisatrice.'" *Review of International Studies* 28:637–56.

Paris Principles. 2007. *The Principles and Guidelines on Children Associated with Armed Forces or Armed Groups.* https://childrenandarmedconflict .un.org/publications/ParisPrinciples_EN.pdf.

Pottier, Johan. 2002. *Re-imagining Rwanda: Conflict, Survival and Disinformation in the Late Twentieth Century.* Cambridge: Cambridge University Press.

Prunier, Gérard. 2009. *Africa's World War: Congo, the Rwandan Genocide, and the Making of a Continental Catastrophe.* New York: Oxford University Press.

Raeymaekers, Timothy. 2010. "Protection for Sale? War and the Transformation of Regulation on the Congo-Ugandan Border." *Development and Change* 41 (4): 563–87.

Rasmussen, Andrew, Leanh Nguyen, John I. D. Wilkinson, Sikhumbuzo Vundla, Sumithra S. Raghavan, Kenneth E. Miller, and Allen S. Keller. 2010. "Rates and Impact of Trauma and Current Stressors among Darfuri Refugees in Eastern Chad." *American Journal of Orthopsychiatry* 80 (2): 223–32.

Reno, William. 1998. *Warlord Politics and African States.* London: Lynne Rienner.

Reyntjens, Filip. 2005. "The Privatisation and Criminalisation of Public Space in the Geopolitics of the Great Lakes Region." *Journal of Modern African Studies* 43 (4): 587–607.

Robinson, Jonathan, and Ethan Yeh. 2011. "Risk-Coping through Sexual Networks: Evidence from Client Transfers in Kenya." Policy Research Working Paper No. WPS 5582. Washington, DC: World Bank.

Roy, Arundhati. 2010. *The Shape of the Beast.* London: Hamish Hamilton.

Rutter, Michael. 2000. "Resilience Reconsidered: Conceptual Considerations, Empirical Findings, and Policy Implications." In *Handbook of Early Childhood Intervention*, edited by J. Shonkoff and S. Meisels, 651–82. Cambridge: Cambridge University Press.

Schopper, Doris. 2014. "Responding to the Needs of Survivors of Sexual Violence: Do We Know What Works?" *International Review of the Red Cross* 96 (894): 585–600.

Scott, James C. 1972. "Patron-Client Politics and Political Change in Southeast Asia." *American Political Science Review* 66 (1): 91–113.

Seay, Laura. 2012. "What's Wrong with Dodd-Frank 1502? Conflict Minerals, Civilian Livelihoods, and the Unintended Consequences of Western Advocacy." Centre for Global Development. https://www.cgdev.org/sites/default/files/1425843_file_Seay_Dodd_Frank_FINAL.pdf.

Seymour, Claudia. 2011a. "Re-conceptualising Child Protection Interventions in Situations of Chronic Conflict: North Kivu, DRC." In *Not Just a Victim: The Child as Catalyst and Witness of Contemporary Africa*, edited by S. Evers, C. Notermans, and E. van Ommering, 223–46. Leiden: Brill.

———. 2011b. "Selective Outrage: The Dangers of Children's DDR in Eastern DRC." *Disarmament Forum* 3:57–66.

———. 2012. "Ambiguous Agencies: Coping and Survival in Eastern DRC." *Children's Geographies* 10 (4): 373–84.

———. 2013. "Young People's Experiences of and Means of Coping with Violence in North and South Kivu Provinces, Democratic Republic of the Congo." PhD diss., University of London.

———. 2014a. "Everyday Violence and War." In *Childhood, Youth and Violence in Global Contexts: Researchers and Practitioners in Dialogue*, edited by K. Wells, E. Burman, H. Montgomery, and A. Watson, 153–72. Hampshire: Palgrave.

———. 2014b. "Zero in the Court of Nine to One: Patronage and Tactical Weakness in Coping with Violence." *Children's Geographies* 12 (3): 268–80.

———. 2017a. "Kids Coping in Congo." In *Geographies of Children and Young People*. Vol. 11, *Conflict, Violence, and Peace*, edited by C. Harker and K. Hörschelmann, 149–68. Heidelberg: Springer.

———. 2017b. "Young People, War, and Interrogating 'Resilience.'" In *Cambridge Encyclopedia of Child Development*, edited by B. Hopkins, E. Geangu, and S. Linkenauger, 862–68. 2nd ed. Cambridge: Cambridge University Press.

Sloterdijk, Peter. 1988. *Critique of Cynical Reason*. Minneapolis: University of Minnesota Press.

Stearns, Jason, and Christoph Vogel. 2015. "The Landscape of Armed Groups in the Eastern Congo." London: Rift Valley Institute.

Summerfield, Derek. 1997. "Legacy of War: Beyond 'Trauma' to the Social Fabric." *Lancet* 349 (9065): 1568.

Tilly, Charles. 1985. "War Making and State Making as Organized Crime." In *Bringing the State Back In*, edited by Peter Evans, Dietrich Rueschemeyer, and Theda Skocpol, 169–86. Cambridge: Cambridge University Press.

Trefon, Theodore. 2004. "Introduction: Reinventing Order." In *Reinventing Order in the Congo: How People Respond to State Failure in Kinshasa*, edited by T. Trefon, 1–19. London and Kampala: Zed Books and Fountain Publishers.

Ungar, Michael. 2008. "Resilience across Cultures." *British Journal of Social Work* 38 (2): 218–35.

UN General Assembly. 1998. *Rome Statute of the International Criminal Court*. Last amended 2010.

United Nations. 1948. "Universal Declaration of Human Rights." http://www.un.org/en/universal-declaration-human-rights/.

————. 2009. *Final Report of the Group of Experts on the DRC, Submitted in Accordance with Paragraph 8 of Security Council Resolution 1857 (2008)*. S/2009/603.

————. 2010. *Report of the Secretary-General on Children and Armed Conflict in the Democratic Republic of the Congo*. S/2010/369.

UN OCHA (United Nations Office for the Coordination of Humanitarian Affairs). 2017a. *Global Humanitarian Overview 2017*. http://www.unocha.org/2017appeal/#p=27.

————. 2017b. "Humanitarian Response Plan 2017–2019." January. https://reliefweb.int/sites/reliefweb.int/files/resources/DRC_HRP_2017.pdf.

————. 2017c. "Response Plans and Appeals Snapshot for 2017." https://fts.unocha.org/appeals/overview/2017.

Utas, Mats. 2005. "Victimcy, Girlfriending, Soldiering: Tactic Agency in a Young Woman's Social Navigation of the Liberian War Zone." *Anthropological Quarterly* 78 (2): 403–30.

Uvin, Peter. 1998. *Aiding Violence: The Development Enterprise in Rwanda*. West Hartford, CT: Kumarian Press.

Verweijin, Judith. 2017. "Luddites in the Congo? Analyzing Violent Responses to the Expansion of Industrial Mining amidst Militarization." *City* 21 (3–4): 466–82.

Vigh, Henrik. 2006. *Navigating Terrains of War: Youth and Soldiering in Guinea-Bissau*. New York: Berghahn Books.

Vlassenroot, Koen. 2000a. "Identity and Insecurity. The Building of Ethnic Agendas in South Kivu." In *Politics of Identity and Economics of*

*Conflict in the Great Lakes Region*, edited by R. Doom and J. Gorus, 263–88. Brussels: VUB University Press.

————. 2000b. "The Promise of Ethnic Conflict: Militarisation and Enclave-Formation in South Kivu." In *Conflict and Ethnicity in Central Africa*, edited by D. Goyvaerts, 59–104. Tokyo: Institute for the Study of Languages and Cultures of Asia and Africa.

————. 2013. "South Kivu: Identity, Territory, and Power in the Eastern Congo." London: Rift Valley Institute.

Vlassenroot, Koen, and Hans Romkema. 2007. "Local Governance and Leadership in Eastern DRC." Commissioned by *Oxfam Novib*.

Wessells, Michael. 2009. "Do No Harm: Toward Contextually Appropriate Psychosocial Support in International Emergencies." *American Psychologist* 64:842–54.

Wessels, Michael, and Alison Strang. 2006. "Religion as Resource and Risk: The Double-Edged Sword for Children in Situations of Armed Conflict." In *A World Turned Upside Down: Social Ecological Approaches to Children in War Zones*, edited by N. Boothby, A. Strang, and M. Wessells, 199–222. Bloomfield, CT: Kumarian Press.

Wolfe, Lauren. 2015. "How Dodd-Frank Is Failing Congo." *Foreign Policy*, 2 February. http://foreignpolicy.com/2015/02/02/how-dodd-frank-is-failing-congo-mining-conflict-minerals/.

Young, Crawford. 1965. *Politics in the Congo: Decolonization and Independence*. Princeton, NJ: Princeton University Press.

# INDEX

abduction, 7, 39, 65, 123, 124, 147
abuse, 6, 7, 8, 29, 36, 58, 59, 60, 80, 81,
    127, 137
accountability, 61, 133, 134, 139, 140
advocacy, 19, 23, 60
"Africa's World War," 3, 34
agency, 17, 83, 85, 86, 124; tactical, 16,
    86, 106
aggression, 66, 110
aid, 1, 13, 15, 17, 19, 65, 102, 106, 107,
    132–135, 137–138, 140
Alliance of Democratic Forces for
    the Liberation of Congo–Zaire
    (AFDL), 20–21, 34, 42, 121–122,
    148n22
ambiguity of coping, 106
Arendt, Hannah, 115
armed groups, 5, 7, 15, 18–19, 23, 25,
    27–28, 60, 78, 146n9, 147nn4,5,
    149nn25,30
Armée de Libération du Rwanda
    (ALiR), 34, 148n22
aspirations, 17, 25, 50, 105, 116, 118,
    120, 126

atrocities, 6, 29–30, 142

Bandura, Albert, 86
Banyamulenge, 32
Banyarwanda, 30, 32–33
Baudouin of Belgium (King), 127
behavior, 45, 85
Belgium/Belgian interests, 2,
    29–30, 32, 94, 96, 128
"beneficiaries," 13, 22, 134, 137–138,
    147n16
Big Man, 100
blame, 4, 13, 37–38, 41, 112–113,
    115, 132
Bourdieu, Pierre, 11–12, 15, 37,
    146nn11,12
Bourgois, Philippe, 9, 116, 145n6
Bukavu, 20–22, 28, 39–40, 42–43,
    51–52, 54–56, 63–65, 77, 99, 102,
    105, 122, 124, 126

Casement, Roger, 30
cassiterite extraction, 84, 139
Chabal, Patrick, 109

child protection, 1–2, 4–5, 7, 10,
    23–24, 27, 44, 46, 59–60, 64
child recruitment, 7, 18–20, 23, 26,
    147nn4,5,6
children, street, 3–4, 77, 80, 88, 91,
    122
"child soldier," 18, 22–23, 27, 137,
    147nn1,4,5
Chödrön, Pema, 142
citizenship, 31–32
cobalt extraction, 139
coercion, 94, 98, 155n22
Cohen, Stanley, 137
coherence, 109–110, 113, 134
Cold War, 2, 94, 96
colonial era, 133, 140
colonial governance/
    administration, 29, 31, 93–94
colonialism, 46, 127–128
coltan extraction, 139
Conférence Nationale
    Souveraine, 32
Congo Free State, 28, 30, 58, 138
Congo Reform Association, 30
Congo Wars, 20, 28, 34–35, 38, 42
Congrès National pour la Défense
    du Peuple (CNDP), 35–36, 40,
    78, 149n24
Conrad, Joseph, 30
coping, 10, 15–16, 41–42, 44,
    46–50, 60, 64, 76–77, 85–87, 92,
    98, 101–102, 104–106, 109, 120–121,
    124–125, 139
copper, 29–30, 139
Core Humanitarian Standard
    on Humanitarian
    Accountability, 134
corruption, 63, 130, 132, 153n8

Daloz, Jean-Pascal, 110
Deaton, Angus, 133, 139
débrouille, la, 83, 86–87, 152n8

de Certeau, Michel, 86
demobilization, 20, 23–25, 41
"democratization" process, 32
denial, 135, 137, 147n4
Department for International
    Development (DFID), 130
dependence, 47, 101, 105–107
de Waal, Alex, 95
diamonds, 30, 139–140
disarmament, demobilization,
    and reintegration (DDR),
    20–26, 29
displacement, 24, 33, 36, 66–67,
    76–79, 91–92, 110, 112, 118, 131, 146,
    148n18
dissent, fear of, 56
dissonance, 15, 17; cognitive, 135
distortion, 14, 62, 65, 81
distrust, 37, 39, 41, 92, 112
"do no harm," 15, 132, 147n15
donor, 13, 19, 26, 62, 65, 134
dowry, 69
due diligence, 139–140
Duffield, Mark, 135

education, 10, 21, 23, 26–27, 47, 65, 85,
    119, 126, 134
elite, 32, 94–96, 111–112, 138
emergency, 5, 8, 61, 100, 131–132
enemy, 40, 113, 124, 142–143
Eriksson Baaz, Maria, 62, 152n8
ethnicity, 27, 32–34, 37, 95
extortion, 53–54, 91, 98
Extractive Industries Transparency
    Initiative (EITI), 139

Fanon, Franz, 129
Farmer, Paul, 50
fear, 6, 8, 12–13, 15, 31, 33, 37,
    39–41, 46, 55–56, 60, 80, 110,
    112, 141–143
forced labor, 29, 58

Forces Armées de la République
  Démocratique du Congo
  (FARDC), 25, 35–36, 39, 54, 58, 61,
  78, 149n25
Forces Armées Rwandaises (FAR),
  33–34
Forces Armées Zairoises (FAZ),
  34, 42
Forces démocratiques de libération
  du Rwanda (FDLR), 34–36,
  38–40, 43, 63, 110, 123–125, 142,
  146n9, 148n22, 149n25
Frankl, Viktor, 109

Galtung, Johan, 49
gender, 16, 63, 66, 68–69, 76, 146
genocide/génocidaire, 33, 38, 112,
  136, 155n15
gold, 25, 30, 83–84, 139, 149n25
Goma, 5–7, 19, 21, 35–36, 55–56, 64,
  79, 88–89, 91
governance, 29, 55, 94, 115, 138, 140
Group of Experts on the DRC, 10,
  146n9

Hochschild, Adam, 29–30, 140
Honwana, Alcinda, 86
hope, 1, 3–4, 7, 14, 16–17, 53, 59–60,
  65, 66, 89, 101–103, 114–115, 118,
  121–123, 125
humanitarian, 8, 15, 17, 29, 36, 106,
  130–134, 136, 140, 147nn16,4
human rights, 6, 8, 10, 30, 36, 56,
  58–60, 114, 126, 134, 141, 146n9,
  156n31
humiliation, 38–39
Hunde, 33, 112–113,
Hutu, 32–33, 36, 38–40, 43, 110, 112

identity, 15–16, 31–34, 37–38, 40–41,
  65, 93, 109–110, 112, 115
impunity, 49, 61, 63, 83

independence, 2, 30–31, 97, 127–128
inequality, 13, 17, 50, 102, 106–107, 112,
  116, 133, 135, 143–144
injustice. *See* justice/injustice
insecurity, 49, 52, 88, 91, 112, 117, 141
Inter-Agency Standing Committee
  (IASC), 134, 136
International Committee of the
  Red Cross (ICRC), 43
International Criminal Court
  (ICC), 23
international law on the
  recruitment and use of
  children, 23
international protection, 13, 17, 58,
  62, 63, 65, 69, 130, 136–137
investigation/investigator, 7, 10, 19,
  22, 36, 38, 59–60, 127, 142, 156n31
Ituri, 59

justice/injustice, 3–14, 49, 56, 61–62,
  102, 113–115, 142

Kabila, Joseph, 34–35, 55
Kabila, Mzee [Laurent], 20, 27, 34,
  148n22
*kadogo*, 27
Kant, Immanuel, 141
Kasai, 131, 152n8
Kasika, 38–39
Keen, David, 8, 138, 147n16, 155n21
Kimberly Process, 139–140
Kimia II, 35
King Leopold II, 2, 29, 30
Kinshasa, 2, 6–7, 9, 11, 20, 35, 64, 98
Kinyarwanda, 38
Kisangani, 2–4, 42
Kivu, 5–6, 11, 15–16, 21, 26–28, 30–35,
  37–40, 42, 46, 49–50, 52–53, 56,
  60–62, 65, 69–70, 77, 83, 85, 88,
  98, 101, 104–106, 109–110, 119, 121,
  126–127, 149n30

Kleinman, Arthur, 68, 120

landownership, 32, 38, 90
law of conservation of violence, 11,
    15, 37, 146n11
Lemarchand, René, 97
lithium-ion batteries, 139
livelihood, 24, 50, 61, 76–77,
    85–87, 93
looting, 78, 91–92, 127
Lumumba, Patrice, 2, 127–128,
    154n23
Lwambo, Desirée, 76

MacGaffey, Janet, 87
malnutrition 130–131
Maniema, 2, 11, 25
Marriage, Zoë, ix, 9, 69, 132,
    137, 143
masculinity, 76
Masisi, 30, 32–34, 77–79, 90, 92, 111,
    114
Mayi-Mayi, 19, 21, 27–28, 34, 38–40,
    110–111, 127
McLean, Paul, 104
meaning, 16, 24–26, 40, 45, 48,
    108–111, 129
migration: forced, 30; migrants,
    29, 142
miners, 14, 139–140
Mission de l'Organisation des
    Nations Unies en République
    démocratique du Congo
    (MONUC), 35, 146n9
Mission de l'Organisation
    des Nations Unies pour la
    stabilisation en République
    démocratique du Congo
    (MONUSCO), 35
Mobutu Sese Seko, 27, 31–32, 34, 43,
    94–96, 98, 152n8
monitoring, 19, 23, 147n4

moral economy, 92, 94
Morel, Edward, 30
Mouvement du 23 mars (M23), 36
Mudundu 40 (M40), 110–111
Mushinga, 25
Mutobo camp (Rwanda), 142

narrative, 11–12, 14, 17–21, 24, 33,
    37–38, 42–43, 65, 76, 80, 83, 91,
    104–105, 111, 114, 116–117, 120–121,
    125, 143, 146n10
Native Authorities, 31, 94
natural resources, 2, 5, 30, 138, 140
nongovernmental organization
    (NGO), 10, 23–24, 62, 64–67,
    69, 79, 84, 113–115, 119, 134–136,
    146n9
Nzeza Bilakila, Anastase, 98

orphans, 27, 103

Paris Principles (Principles
    and Guidelines on Children
    Associated with Armed Forces
    and Armed Groups), 23–24,
    147n5, 148n7
patrimonialism, 93, 95, 98
patronage, 16, 92–99, 101–105
patron-client, 95–97, 105
peacekeeping, 1–3, 36, 145n2
perpetrator, 19, 37, 40, 76, 110, 124, 127
pillage, 39, 59, 92, 110, 127
political economy, 8–9, 11, 17, 63, 94,
    138, 140, 147n16, 155n21
post-traumatic stress disorder
    (PTSD), 44, 150n8
poverty, 3–4, 15, 26–27, 44, 47,
    49–52, 62, 76, 78, 80, 84–86,
    90–92, 98, 101, 107, 112, 116, 118,
    135, 156n31
power, 5, 8, 17, 28, 32–33, 39, 50, 53–57,
    77, 85, 89, 93–94, 97–98, 101–102,

104–106, 109, 112–113, 116, 118–120, 124, 128, 139–140, 158
precarity, 3, 141
predation, 96, 98,
prostitution, 79–80
protective environment, 137
protest, 37, 53–56, 129
Prunier, Gérard, 3, 27, 96, 145n3
psychology, 9, 15–16, 44–48
psychosocial support, 61–62, 66, 113, 147n15

rape, 16, 38–41, 43–44, 49, 52, 56, 58–67, 69, 76, 80–82, 122, 124–125, 127, 137, 147n4, 151n2
Rassemblement congolais pour la démocratie (RCD), 20–22, 34–35, 38–40, 43–44, 110, 123
reintegration, 20–22, 24–26, 61–62, 147n5
repression, 55, 98, 129
resilience, 15, 46–48, 95, 150n11
resistance, 2, 12, 53, 68, 81, 109–110, 120, 124, 129, 141–143
"Responsibility to Protect" framework, 136
risk, 10, 13, 45–47, 52, 56, 67, 79–80, 85, 90, 107, 113, 116, 118, 121, 131
Rome Statute, 23, 147n6
Roy, Arundhati, 136
Rutshuru, 6, 30, 32–34
Rwanda, 3, 11, 22, 30–35, 38–40, 112, 136, 142, 146n9, 149nn24,25

safety net, 77, 88
School of Oriental and African Studies, x, 9
Scott, James C., 92–93
sex, transactional, 16, 76–77, 79
sexual violence, 7, 14, 16, 19, 36, 58, 60, 62–63, 65–66, 68–69, 76, 81–82, 146n13, 147n4, 151n2, 152n26

shame, 41, 66, 76
Shantideva, vi, 13, 144
Simba rebellion, 2
slaves, 29–30, 63, 128, 140
Sloterdijk, Peter, 141–142
state-citizen contract, 133
Stern, Maria, 62
structural violence, 15–16, 49–50, 53, 68, 91–92, 101, 116–117
structures of violence, 27, 50, 53, 55–56, 118, 120–121, 137, 139
subjugation, 29, 66, 107
submission, 53, 55, 57, 108, 116, 120–121, 127
sub-Saharan Africa, 31, 86, 94, 96, 101, 103–104
suffering, 64, 68, 128, 132
Sukola II, 36
social support, 3, 90–91, 97–98, 101, 113
survival, 4, 14–16, 22, 24, 26, 37, 49–51, 53, 55–56, 62–63, 66, 76, 78, 79, 83–84, 86–88, 92–93, 97–98, 100–104, 106–107, 120–121, 125, 139
Sustainable Development Goals, 2030 Agenda of the, 135

tactical agency, 16, 86
tantalum extraction, 139
terrorists, 142–143
tin extraction, 139
torture, 4, 29, 127
trauma, 44–47, 68
tungsten extraction, 139
Tutsi, 32–34, 38, 40, 42–43, 112

Umoja Wetu, 35
unemployment, 27, 49, 90, 92, 114
Ungar, Michael, 48
United Nations (UN), 1–3, 5, 10, 19, 23, 34–36, 59–61, 67, 131–136, 141–142, 145n2, 146nn7,9, 147n4, 156n31

UNICEF, 18, 131
Universal Declaration of Human
  Rights, 141
Utas, Mats, 86, 106

victimcy, 106
victim-perpetrator discourses, 37
victims, 14, 19, 37, 45, 58, 60–63,
  65–66, 81–82, 105–107, 111, 135, 137
vulnerability, 31, 46, 47, 77, 101,
  106–107, 134, 136–137

Walungu, 24, 121, 123
weakness, tactical, 16, 102

well-being, 48–49, 109
Williams, George Washington, 29
witchcraft, 4
witnesses, 1–2, 6, 15, 24, 26, 29, 38,
  45, 51, 56, 59, 61, 78, 100, 108, 128,
  146n9
wolframite extraction, 139
World Food Programme, 67
World Humanitarian Summit,
  135

Young, Crawford, 94, 97

Zaire, 20, 87, 94–97

CALIFORNIA SERIES IN PUBLIC
ANTHROPOLOGY

The California Series in Public Anthropology
emphasizes the anthropologist's role as an
engaged intellectual. It continues anthropology's
commitment to being an ethnographic witness,
to describing, in human terms, how life is lived
beyond the borders of many readers' experiences. But it also adds a commitment, through
ethnography, to reframing the terms of public
debate—transforming received, accepted understandings of social issues with new insights, new
framings.

*Series Editor: Robert Borofsky (Hawaii Pacific
University)*

*Contributing Editors: Philippe Bourgois (University of
Pennsylvania), Paul Farmer (Partners In Health),
Alex Hinton (Rutgers University), Carolyn Nordstrom
(University of Notre Dame), and Nancy Scheper-
Hughes (UC Berkeley)*

*University of California Press Editor: Naomi
Schneider*

1.  *Twice Dead: Organ Transplants and the Reinvention of Death*,
    by Margaret Lock

2.  *Birthing the Nation: Strategies of Palestinian Women in Israel*, by Rhoda
    Ann Kanaaneh (with a foreword by Hanan Ashrawi)

3.  *Annihilating Difference: The Anthropology of Genocide*, edited by
    Alexander Laban Hinton (with a foreword by Kenneth Roth)

4.  *Pathologies of Power: Health, Human Rights, and the New War on the
    Poor*, by Paul Farmer (with a foreword by Amartya Sen)

5.  *Buddha Is Hiding: Refugees, Citizenship, the New America*, by Aihwa Ong

6.  *Chechnya: Life in a War-Torn Society*, by Valery Tishkov (with a
    foreword by Mikhail S. Gorbachev)

7. *Total Confinement: Madness and Reason in the Maximum Security Prison*, by Lorna A. Rhodes

8. *Paradise in Ashes: A Guatemalan Journey of Courage, Terror, and Hope*, by Beatriz Manz (with a foreword by Aryeh Neier)

9. *Laughter Out of Place: Race, Class, Violence, and Sexuality in a Rio Shantytown*, by Donna M. Goldstein

10. *Shadows of War: Violence, Power, and International Profiteering in the Twenty-First Century*, by Carolyn Nordstrom

11. *Why Did They Kill? Cambodia in the Shadow of Genocide*, by Alexander Laban Hinton (with a foreword by Robert Jay Lifton)

12. *Yanomami: The Fierce Controversy and What We Can Learn from It*, by Robert Borofsky

13. *Why America's Top Pundits Are Wrong: Anthropologists Talk Back*, edited by Catherine Besteman and Hugh Gusterson

14. *Prisoners of Freedom: Human Rights and the African Poor*, by Harri Englund

15. *When Bodies Remember: Experiences and Politics of AIDS in South Africa*, by Didier Fassin

16. *Global Outlaws: Crime, Money, and Power in the Contemporary World*, by Carolyn Nordstrom

17. *Archaeology as Political Action*, by Randall H. McGuire

18. *Counting the Dead: The Culture and Politics of Human Rights Activism in Colombia*, by Winifred Tate

19. *Transforming Cape Town*, by Catherine Besteman

20. *Unimagined Community: Sex, Networks, and AIDS in Uganda and South Africa*, by Robert J. Thornton

21. *Righteous Dopefiend*, by Philippe Bourgois and Jeff Schonberg

22. *Democratic Insecurities: Violence, Trauma, and Intervention in Haiti*, by Erica Caple James

23. *Partner to the Poor: A Paul Farmer Reader*, by Paul Farmer, edited by Haun Saussy (with a foreword by Tracy Kidder)

24. *I Did It to Save My Life: Love and Survival in Sierra Leone*, by Catherine E. Bolten

25. *My Name Is Jody Williams: A Vermont Girl's Winding Path to the Nobel Peace Prize*, by Jody Williams

26. *Reimagining Global Health: An Introduction,* by Paul Farmer, Jim Yong Kim, Arthur Kleinman, and Matthew Basilico

27. *Fresh Fruit, Broken Bodies: Migrant Farmworkers in the United States,* by Seth M. Holmes, PhD, MD

28. *Illegality, Inc.: Clandestine Migration and the Business of Bordering Europe,* by Ruben Andersson

29. *To Repair the World: Paul Farmer Speaks to the Next Generation,* by Paul Farmer

30. *Blind Spot: How Neoliberalism Infiltrated Global Health,* by Salmaan Keshavjee (with a foreword by Paul Farmer)

31. *Driving after Class: Anxious Times in an American Suburb,* by Rachel Heiman

32. *The Spectacular Favela: Violence in Modern Brazil,* by Erika Robb Larkins

33. *When I Wear My Alligator Boots: Narco-Culture in the U.S. Mexico Borderlands,* by Shaylih Muehlmann

34. *Jornalero: Being a Day Laborer in the USA,* by Juan Thomas Ordóñez

35. *A Passion for Society: How We Think about Human Suffering,* by Iain Wilkinson and Arthur Kleinman

36. *The Land of Open Graves: Living and Dying on the Migrant Trail,* by Jason De León (with photographs by Michael Wells)

37. *Living with Difference: How to Build Community in a Divided World,* by Adam Seligman, Rahel Wasserfall, and David Montgomery

38. *Scratching Out a Living: Latinos, Race, and Work in the Deep South,* by Angela Stuesse

39. *Returned: Going and Coming in an Age of Deportation,* by Deborah A. Boehm

40. *They Leave Their Kidneys in the Fields: Injury, Illness, and Illegality among U.S. Farmworkers,* by Sarah Bronwen Horton

41. *Threshold: Emergency Responders on the U.S.-Mexico Border,* by Ieva Jusionyte

42. *Lives in Transit: Violence and Intimacy on the Migrant Journey,* by Wendy A. Vogt

43. *The Myth of International Protection: War and Survival in Congo,* by Claudia Seymour